CLASS STATE AND CRIME

On the theory and practice of criminal justice

RICHARD QUINNEY

David McKay Company, Inc.
New York

CLASS, STATE, AND CRIME:
On the Theory and Practice of Criminal Justice

MANUFACTURED IN THE UNITED STATES OF AMERICA

Developmental Editor: Edward Artinian
Editorial and Design Supervisor: Nicole Benevento
Design: Pencils Portfolio, Inc.
Production and Manufacturing Supervisor: Donald W. Strauss
Composition: Fuller Typesetting of Lancaster
Printing and Binding: Haddon Craftsmen

Library of Congress Cataloging in Publication Data

Quinney, Richard.
Class, state, and crime.

Includes index.
1. Crime and criminals–Economic aspects. 2. Capitalism. 3. Criminal justice, Administration of–United States. I. Title.
HV6171.Q54 364 76–58840
ISBN 0–679–30334–0
ISBN 0–679–30342–1 pbk.

PREFACE

Criminal justice has emerged as a principal feature of modern, advanced capitalist society. When a society cannot solve the social problems of its own creation, policies for the control of the population must be devised and implemented. The purpose of this book is to understand the meaning of criminal justice in theory and practice as found in the United States.

To understand criminal justice we must investigate the larger issues of the historical development of capitalism, the material basis of crime (including both crime control and criminality), the class structure of advanced capitalism, the role of the capitalist state, and the political economy of criminal justice. Eventually our task is to document the development of control policies in the history of the United States in relation to the economic and political development of the nation. But before that could be attempted, theoretical questions have to be raised and resolved in some manner. This book is the result of that effort.

The contradiction of criminal justice today is that the state must provide a framework for continuing capitalist accumulation and at the same time perform legitimation functions for the existing order, and the state increasingly finds it difficult to provide the resources for these services. While there is a growing surplus population produced by the political economy of advanced capitalism, a population that must be serviced and controlled, the financial resources increasingly become limited. The criminal justice policies of recent years must be seen in the context of this contradiction. Criminal justice has traditionally been one part of the policies of the welfare state. But as the liberal welfare state fails to solve its own contradictions, its demise becomes imminent, and criminal justice takes on new forms. That a new model of criminal justice—one based explicitly on punishment—has emerged is a reflection of the economic and political crisis of late, advanced capitalism. This takes on further meaning as the class struggle is heightened and increasingly politicized in the course of these developments.

The future of criminal justice will be determined by changes in the objective conditions of the last stages of capitalism and by the rising political consciousness of the working class, especially by that expanding portion of the working class now being relegated to a surplus population. Currently we are developing a theory and a practice for a transitional society, one that is moving from late capitalism to early socialism. In the transition, popular forms of action —beyond state-sponsored programs of criminal justice— are emerging. Popular justice is the immediate alternative to criminal justice. What forms will develop in the future will become evident only as we move to a socialist society. To understand criminal justice is to join in the struggle for a new society.

CONTENTS

TABLES

FIGURES

CLASS
STATE AND
CRIME

1 CRIMINAL JUSTICE IN CAPITALIST SOCIETY

Justice begins in contradiction. The notion itself–in theoretical isolation–is an absolute statement of an ideal. Justice supposedly transcends everyday existence. In practice, however, justice is inevitably shaped by social reality. Justice is rarely realized.

But the contradiction goes even deeper. The theory of justice is rooted in social existence. Whatever the particular notion of justice, wherever practiced, justice as a concept is materially based. The transcendent ideal rests on a concrete historical foundation. Justice is an integral part of the social, economic, and political structure of a society. Rather than being removed from the material world, justice plays a crucial role in establishing and perpetuating social order.

Nowhere is justice more important–in both theory and practice–than in capitalist society. The concept of justice has evolved with the development of capitalism. At each stage of economic development, the particular notion of justice has been tied to the material basis of production, playing a part in securing the existing order. The struggle between classes, central to developing capitalism, is regulated by capitalist justice. Justice in capitalist society, today as always, is an ideological and practical instrument in class struggle.

Thus, a consideration of justice begins in a materialist analysis. We might well ask, given a Marxist understanding of the meaning of justice, whether "justice" is necessary. A transcendent ideal of justice eventually may be dialectically important in the development of new social and economic forms, including the emergence of socialist society. But the immediate fact is that capitalist justice secures the capitalist system. In an understanding of capitalist justice, especially in relation to crime, we can demystify our history and current experiences and move to a theory and practice that will realize a socialist society.

CAPITALIST JUSTICE

Although "justice" can assume different and even diverse principles, the notion of justice that we conventionally know is an accumulation of ideas that have formed in the course of the development of capitalism. However mystified, justice is a social norm that is a directive for guiding human action.[1] Actions are judged in terms of the directive; and justice is dispensed according to some notion of equality for people in similar situations. But as social norm, following our Greek heritage, justice complies with the in-

1. Otto A. Bird, *The Idea of Justice* (New York: Frederick A. Praeger, 1967), pp. 11–13.

terests of the stronger, mainly the needs of the ruling class as expressed in law.

Although justice is to be applied to individual cases, the general objective is the promotion of social order. As thus conceived, individualistic needs and social order are combined to form the "healthy" whole:

> The problem of justice is closely related to the problem of a healthy order of society. It is concerned with the healthfulness of the parts as well as with sound condition of the whole. These two aspects of justice are, of course, inseparable. If the needs and aspirations of the individuals composing society are reasonably taken care of by the system of justice, and if reciprocal concern for the health of the social body exists among the members of society, there is a good chance that a harmonious and flourishing society will be the result.[2]

And in capitalist society the healthy order is the one that benefits the capitalist class, the class that owns and controls the productive process. Capitalist justice is by the capitalist class, for the capitalist class, and against the working class.

To our contemporary mind, questions of justice are generally restricted to a consideration of "equal justice"—and severely limited even within that realm. Again following the Greek path, justice originates in the belief that equals should be treated equally *and* unequals unequally.[3] In practice this has come to mean that discrimination in dispensing justice for infractions should not occur beyond that justified by relevant differences. This leaves wide open such questions as the concrete meaning of equality, the

2. Edgar Bodenheimer, *Treatise on Justice* (New York: Philosophical Library, 1967), p. 8.
3. Morris Ginsberg, *On Justice in Society* (Baltimore: Penguin Books, 1965), p. 7.

social reality of equality and inequality, the existence of class conflict and state power, and the struggle for a better society beyond a narrow sense of justice.

Justice in contemporary capitalist society equates the limited idea of equal justice with the formulation and administration of positive law. Capitalist justice, in other words, is made concrete in the establishment of legal order. All notions of goodness, evil, and the earthly kingdom become embodied in capitalist law. And in everyday life the questions of justice are confined to whether or not the law is arbitrarily administered. Justice is grounded not in some alternative idea of the social good or natural order, but in the survival needs of the capitalist system. Judgment is now in the hands of legal agencies of the capitalist state. Legality and the "rational" administration of the law have become the capitalist symbol of justice.

In recent years, in response to a crisis in the legitimation of capitalist institutions as well as the more general crisis in the capitalist system, there has been renewed interest in the concept of justice. Diverse presentations such as John Rawls' *A Theory of Justice* and Robert Nozick's *Anarchy, State, and Utopia* attest to the chaos in our thinking about justice.[4] It is important to note, first, that both philosophical treatises are in defense of some version of capitalism. Serious academic attention is being directed to the philosophical underpinnings for modern capitalist society. Marxist critiques, theories, and practices, however, are beginning to emerge.

The current theories of justice are rooted in the moral and political problems generated by advanced capitalism. The solutions presented by Rawls and Nozick are within the

4. John Rawls, *A Theory of Justice* (Cambridge, Mass.: Harvard University Press, 1971); Robert Nozick, *Anarchy, State, and Utopia* (New York: Basic Books, 1974).

liberal bourgeois tradition. Nevertheless, while Nozick espouses a pure form of laissez-faire capitalism, today called "libertarianism," Rawls bases his discussion on a philosophy of the liberal welfare state.[5] Justice for Nozick is a world of separate individuals, with individual rights, who exist and act irrespective of being in society. From this "state of nature" follows the right to property, a free market of competition, and very little interference from a "minimal state." Rawls' theory of justice, while similarly attentive to the freedom of individuals to achieve their own good, considers the principles necessary to govern the distribution of the means to achieve individual goods. It is the modern welfare state that assures and regulates this distribution.

Rawls bases his theory of justice on a hypothetical condition where rational people live in an "original position." There is consensus on the principles of living together, a liberal agreement of what is important for the fulfillment of individual goals. Omitted from this individualistic view are the realities of class conflict, exploitation, and ruling-class power.[6] Moreover, the "original position" is neutral toward values that emphasize cooperative relations between people and collective or communal activity. Opposed is any conception of society that sees human life as the collective achievement of a social good.

The liberal version of justice in capitalist society selectively and necessarily excludes a socialist vision of social order. The essence of liberalism is a society made up of autonomous units that associate only to further individual

5. A review that focuses on the political implications of these philosophies is presented in Allen Graubard, "Liberty and/or Justice for All," *Working Papers for a New Society* 3 (Summer 1975): 57–59, 73–77.
6. See Thomas Nagel, "Rawls on Justice," *Philosophical Review* 82 (April 1973): 220–34; and Richard Miller, "Rawls and Marxism," *Philosophy and Public Affairs* 3 (Winter 1974): 167–91.

ends. Capitalist market relations are the paradigm for justice in the liberal philosophy of justice.[7] An alternative theory of justice in society, one based on cooperative and collective action, must be found in socialist philosophy. This is a philosophy that is worked out in the course of socialist practice.

THE RISE OF CRIMINAL JUSTICE

The capitalist notion of justice is most explicitly represented in the application to the problem of crime. Since the middle 1960s, with the increasing crisis of capitalism, official and public attention has focused on rising crime and its control. A solution to the crisis became simply that of fighting the domestic enemy–*crime*. In a presidential message to Congress in 1965, the "war on crime" was launched. The President declared that "we must arrest and reverse the trend toward lawlessness," suggesting that "crime has become a malignant enemy in America's midst."[8] Congress responded by enacting the Omnibus Crime Control and Safe Streets Act, noting in its opening statement the scale of the project: "Congress finds that the high incidence of crime in the United States threatens the peace, security and general welfare of the Nation and its citizens. To prevent crime and to insure the greater safety of the people, law enforcement efforts must be better coor-

7. Brian Barry, *The Liberal Theory of Justice: A Critical Examination of the Principal Doctrines in a Theory of Justice by John Rawls* (New York: Oxford University Press, 1972).
8. "Crime, Its Prevalence, and Measures of Prevention," Message from the President of the United States, House of Representatives, 89th Congress, 8 March 1965, Document No. 103.

dinated, intensified, and made more effective at all levels of government."[9]

A new form of crime control was being established in capitalist society. Not only was the war on crime intensified by legislation, presidential commissions, and policy research by liberal academicians, but the capitalist state was now instituting a new system of domestic control. Especially with the newly created federal agency, the Law Enforcement Assistance Administration (LEAA), with appropriations amounting to millions of dollars, all levels of government were involved in planning and implementing an apparatus to secure the existing capitalist order.[10]

In the process, a new terminology has been created: that of *criminal justice*. Theoretically the terminology updates the ideology of "law and order." But adding to the conventional image, the terminology of criminal justice recognizes the new emphasis being placed on maintaining the existing order through the tools and agencies of the capitalist state. In practice criminal justice represents an innovation in control, indeed, the establishment of a new system of control, a "criminal justice system." With the euphemism of criminal justice, within a decade a new system of control has been established and (at the same time) justified. Today we are all attuned in one way or another to criminal justice.

With the war on crime and the development of a new criminal justice system there has emerged the new field of criminal justice research and education. The need for criminal justice research was expressed by the President's Com-

9. "Omnibus Crime Control and Safe Streets Act," Public Law 90–351, *United States Statutes at Large, 1968* (Washington, D.C.: U.S. Government Printing Office, 1969), 82:197.

10. See Richard Quinney, *Critique of Legal Order: Crime Control in Capitalist Society* (Boston: Little, Brown, 1974), esp. pp. 95–135.

mission on Law Enforcement and Administration of Justice in 1967:

> The Commission has found and discussed many needs of law enforcement and the administration of criminal justice. But what it has found to be the greatest need is the need to know. America has learned the uses of exploration and discovery and knowledge in shaping and controlling its physical environment, in protecting its health, in furthering its national security, and in countless other ways. . . . But this revolution of scientific discovery has largely bypassed the problems of crime and crime control. . . . There is virtually no subject connected with crime or criminal justice into which further research is unnecessary.[11]

Congress responded by establishing the National Institute of Law Enforcement and Criminal Justice within LEAA, through a provision in the Omnibus Crime Control and Safe Streets Act of 1968. The National Institute provides a mechanism for initiating and coordinating criminal justice research on a national level, providing resources beyond those already furnished by other federal agencies, such as the Center for Studies of Crime and Delinquency at the National Institute of Mental Health.

Since its creation in 1968, the activities of the National Institute of Law Enforcement and Criminal Justice have grown considerably in scope: "The Institute's work encompasses research aimed at developing methods to reduce specific crimes, basic research into the nature and causes of crime and delinquency, the evaluation of crime reduction programs, the application of scientific and technological advances to criminal justice, and the transfer and dissemination of research findings to criminal justice agencies around

11. President's Commission on Law Enforcement and Administration of Justice, *The Challenge of Crime in a Free Society* (Washington, D.C.: U.S. Government Printing Office, 1967), p. 273.

the country and throughout the world."[12] The Crime Control Act of 1973 further expanded the role of the National Institute by giving it authority to develop training programs for criminal justice personnel, to create an international clearinghouse for the collection and dissemination of criminal justice information, including data on acts of crime, and to evaluate LEAA programs and projects. The budget of the National Institute has risen from $3 million in 1968 to over $40 million in the mid-1970s. The criminal justice system in the United States is increasingly being rationalized through the introduction and application of a new scientific technology of criminal justice.

Recognizing that the new technology requires an educated and indoctrinated personnel, academic programs in criminal justice have developed rapidly in the last decade. The Crime Control and Safe Streets Act of 1968 authorized LEAA to make grants and loans to criminal justice personnel and to those who plan to be employed in the criminal justice system. The major education program of LEAA, called the Law Enforcement Education Program (LEEP), provides financial support for the college education of persons employed in law enforcement, courts, corrections, and other criminal justice agencies. Since the beginning of the program, approximately 200,000 students have received financial support from LEEP. The program has grown from 20,602 students in 485 colleges and universities to more than 95,000 students in 1,036 schools.[13] Funding has increased from $6.5 million in 1969 to more than $84 million in 1976 for manpower development. LEAA provides funds for criminal justice graduate pro-

12. Law Enforcement Assistance Administration, *Sixth Annual Report of LEAA* (Washington, D.C.: U.S. Government Printing Office, 1974), p. 58.
13. Ibid., p. 66.

grams, sponsors a graduate research fellowship program, and provides funds to enable college students to work in criminal justice agencies, thus promoting an interest in future criminal justice careers.

These federally funded programs also have had the effect of changing the social sciences, going beyond the specific criminal justice education. Courses that consider the phenomenon of crime, such as criminology courses taught in sociology departments, now give more attention to criminal justice, and in many cases have adopted the criminal justice and administrative perspective.[14] Furthermore, some criminal justice programs have grown out of former social science courses. At some colleges and universities courses in the sociology of crime have been shifted to the criminal justice curriculum. The modern move to criminal justice, in other words, is shaping the nature of our lives and minds in many ways. We are in an age of criminal justice.

The criminal justice movement is thus understood as a state-initiated and state-supported effort to rationalize mechanisms of social control. The larger purpose is to secure a capitalist order that is in grave crisis, likely in its final stage of development. The criminal justice system will surely be modified in response to further problems generated by late capitalism. Technological as well as ideological solutions will be attempted. There will be greater efforts at criminal

14. See Donald J. Newman, *Introduction to Criminal Justice* (Philadelphia: J. B. Lippincott, 1975), pp. vii–xiv. Also Joseph J. Senna, "Criminal Justice Higher Education–Its Growth and Directions," *Crime and Delinquency* 20 (October 1974): 389–97; Fred I. Klyman and Thomas A. Karman, "A Perspective for Graduate-Level Education in Criminal Justice, *Crime and Delinquency* 20 (October 1974): 398–404.

justice planning, to develop a comprehensive system of criminal justice.[15] Not only will the traditional agencies of the law be systematized, involving the police and the courts, but more emphasis will be on the prevention of crime. A new technology of crime prevention will likely emerge. Already, as indicated in the 1975 report of the National Advisory Commission on Criminal Justice Standards and Goals, an LEAA-sponsored commission, alternatives to the existing criminal justice agencies are being proposed and implemented.[16] The Commission advises, in particular, alternatives to legal processing outside of the criminal justice system. Cases are to be diverted from the courts, and new agencies ("non-criminal-justice institutions") are to deal with cases formerly handled by the police and the courts. This leaves the criminal justice system free to deal with serious offenses against the state and the economy and at the same time makes a wide range of social behavior subject to surveillance and control by the state. Criminal justice is expanding, and in the process will make further changes to provide greater control within the capitalist order.

Finally, the state is initiating the "participation" of the citizenry in crime control. Public concern about crime is being channeled into approved kinds of responses. The public is thus being enlisted into the criminal justice system.

15. See, for example, James E. Frank and Frederic L. Faust, "A Conceptual Framework for Criminal Justice Planning," *Criminology* 13 (August 1975): 271–96; Daniel Glaser, *Strategic Criminal Justice Planning,* National Institute of Mental Health, Center for Studies of Crime and Delinquency (Washington, D.C.: U.S. Government Printing Office, 1975).
16. National Advisory Commission on Criminal Justice Standards and Goals, *A National Strategy to Reduce Crime* (New York: Avon, 1975).

The newly created Citizens' Initiative Program of LEAA emphasizes several ways in which the public can become involved:

–Developing ways to assist crime victims
–Encouraging public education programs on all criminal justice system functions
–Increasing public awareness of citizen responsibility for crime control and crime prevention
–Alleviating crime causes through citizen action programs
–Implementing community-based offender reintegration projects
–Planning comprehensive crime prevention strategies
–Encouraging citizen involvement in the criminal justice system, particularly in witness or juror environment projects [17]

We are told that in cities large and small, hundreds of thousands of citizens are organizing to fight crime, doing such specific things as (1) encouraging victims to report all crimes and testifying against the accused, (2) helping the police by patrolling their own neighborhoods, (3) serving as auxiliary police or sheriffs' reserves, (4) keeping watch on neighbors' homes, (5)reporting suspicious activities in their neighborhoods, (6) securing their own homes from crime, (7) educating children to obey the laws and respect the police, (8) keeping watch on courts to spot judges who are soft on crime, and (9) demanding stronger anticrime laws.[18]

17. Law Enforcement Assistance Administration, *LEAA Focus on Citizens' Initiative* (Washington, D.C.: U.S. Government Printing Office, 1975), p. 4.
18. "War on Crime by Fed-Up Citizens," *U.S. News & World Report*, 29 September 1975, pp. 19–22.

We are all to be a part of the criminal justice system. However, the official programs for citizen participation are being contradicted by initiatives that are being taken by people outside of state-sponsored programs. Built into the state efforts at citizen participation is a dialectic that supports autonomous community action removed from state control. Developing alongside the criminal justice system is a grass-roots approach that is beyond the design of the state. The dialectic undoubtedly will advance in coming years. Community actions themselves will be subject to criminal justice.

CRIME AND PUNISHMENT

That particular tradition of social theory whose formulations uphold and perpetuate the established order is currently undergoing revision. The social, political, and economic events of recent years in the United States–and in the whole of the capitalist world–have forced the social theorist to new formulations about the nature of the crisis in social order. At the same time an emerging Marxian theory provides a critique of the crisis in capitalist societies, as well as creating a politics, conventional social theory seeks intellectual and policy solutions that attempt to preserve the dying order.

One of the crucial points at which conventional social theory is being revised is in reference to crime and criminal justice. Crime has come to symbolize the ultimate crack in the armor of the existing social order. And given the modern pessimism that social problems cannot really be solved –without drastically altering the established order–controls must be instituted to protect "our society." Recent thinking about crime, combined with proposed policies, therefore have to be taken seriously as containing notions for the revision of social theory.

Several books about crime and criminal justice, and considerable empirical research, are providing important ideas for the formulations that would secure the capitalist order. These works bridge the interests of a range of social scientists, including sociologists, economists, criminologists, legal behavioralists, and policy scientists. That most of these books are grounded in a moral philosophy, attending particularly to a notion of justice, makes their appearance even more important; the best of social theory is necessarily founded on moral and philosophical premises. What is emerging for the conventional social theorists, then, the theorists who would preserve the established system, is a new philosophy and likely a revised social theory for advanced capitalist society.

Most social theorists postulate some notion about the nature of human nature. For James Q. Wilson, in his book *Thinking About Crime,* a "clear and sober understanding of the nature of man" is required not only for purposes of theory but for "the proper design of public policies." [19] Human nature and subsequent policy are simply conceived: "Wicked people exist"—"Nothing avails except to set them apart from innocent people." [20] Crime, in all its reification, thus provides the metaphor for our human nature; crime represents human nature in its "less attractive" form. Thinking about crime as Wilson does is to advance one possible notion of being human and one possible way of controlling that nature.

Moreover, being wicked (and criminal) is a *rational* choice. In all our affiairs, following this image, we are self-

19. James Q. Wilson, *Thinking About Crime* (New York: Basic Books, 1975), p. xi.
20. Ibid., p. 209.

interested people rationally pursuing what is best for ourselves and, perhaps, our families. We are rational in the capitalistic, individual and economic, sense. And our criminality, according to the recent economic statement on crime, explicitly stated in an influential article by Gary S. Becker, is utilitarian: "A person commits an offense if the expected utility to him exceeds the utility he could get by using his time and resources at other activities." [21] The obvious solution coming from the rational-utilitarian model is to deter crime by raising the risks of crime.

The notion of the capitalist (rational and utilitarian) individual thus gives support to the renewed interest in *deterrence* as social policy. Current research by sociologists seeks to establish the importance of "certainty" and "swiftness" of punishment in deterring crime.[22] In addition there

21. Gary S. Becker, "Crime and Punishment: An Economic Approach," *Journal of Political Economy* 76 (March–April 1968): 176. Also see the writings in Gary S. Becker and William M. Landes, eds., *Essays in the Economics of Crime and Punishment* (New York: National Bureau of Economic Research, 1974); and Simon Rottenberg, ed., *The Economics of Crime and Punishment* (Washington, D.C.: American Enterprise Institute for Policy Research, 1973).
22. For example, Theodore G. Chiricos and Gordon P. Waldo, "Punishment and Crime: An Examination of Some Empirical Evidence," *Social Problems* 18 (Fall 1970): 200–217; Maynard L. Erickson and Jack P. Gibbs, "Specific Versus General Properties of Legal Punishments and Deterrence," *Social Science Quarterly* 56 (December 1975): 390–97; Charles H. Logan, "General Deterrent Effects of Imprisonment," *Social Forces* 51 (September 1972): 64–73; Robert V. Stover and Don W. Brown, "Understanding Compliance and Non-Compliance with Law: The Contributions of Utility Theory," *Social Science Quarterly* 56 (December 1975): 363–75; Charles R. Tittle, "Crime Rates and Legal Sanctions," *Social Problems* 16 (Spring 1969): 409–23; Charles R. Tittle and Charles H. Logan, "Sanctions and Deviance: Evidence and Remaining Questions," *Law and Society Review* 7 (Spring 1973): 371–92.

are the legal and philosophical works, such as *Deterrence* by Franklin E. Zimring and Gordon J. Hawkins.[23] In this book, legal scholars lend their weight to the new utilitarianism, arguing that the purpose of the criminal sanction is to deter criminal acts and that this is accomplished by declaring and administering pain in cases of noncompliance to the legal code of the existing order. While the book contains an elaborate framework for empirically determining the "deterrent effect" of punishment, the overall thrust is to make deterrence (i.e., *punishment*) "morally tolerable." Although the traditional dichotomy between liberal and conservative may yet distinguish responses to some issues, when it comes to crime and criminal policy, the distinction is of little importance. The practical possibilities of punishment characterize the modern debate. What binds Wilson's thinking to the scheme of Zimring and Hawkins, and these works with Ernest van Den Haag's conservative argument in his new book explicitly called *Punishing Criminals,* is the contemporary justification for further instituting punishment in the capitalist state.[24] As the "rehabilitation" ideal proves itself bankrupt in practice, liberals and conservatives alike (all within the capitalist hegemony) resort to the utilitarianism of pain.

So it is that new emphasis is given to the *prison* as a place of punishment. Norval Morris, dean of the University of Chicago Law School, in his recent book *The Future of Imprisonment,* furnishes "general principles under which imprisonment may be part of a rational criminal justice

23. Franklin E. Zimring and Gordon J. Hawkins, *Deterrence: The Legal Threat in Crime Control* (Chicago: University of Chicago Press, 1973).
24. Ernest van Den Haag, *Punishing Criminals: Concerning a Very Old and Painful Question* (New York: Basic Books, 1975).

system."[25] While some forms of rehabilitation may be attempted within the prison of the future, mainly in a "facilitative" capacity, the principal objective of the prison is to punish the criminal. Morris thus writes: "In my view, penal purposes are properly retributive and deterrent. To add reformative purposes to that mix–as a purpose of the sanction as distinct from a collateral aspiration–produces neither clemency nor justice."[26] Morris then tries to justify imprisonment as a rational form of control, providing a moral as well as rational framework for incarceration. Justice and rationality are thus linked.

With works and ideas such as these, combined with the sociological research that seemingly gives semblance of support, we have the reconstruction of a reality that takes as given the existing social order. Rather than suggesting an alternative order, one based on a different conception of human nature, political economy, and social justice, we are presented with schemes that merely justify further repression within the established order. The solutions being offered can only exacerbate the conditions of our existence.

It is with such convoluted rationality that Wilson turns his thinking to an epistemology of causal and policy analysis. In this discussion Wilson lays bare the elements of the new utilitarianism that increasingly characterizes both government policy and social theory. After reviewing traditional theorizing about crime, Wilson argues that such theorizing about the "root causes" of crime fails because it

25. Norval Morris, *Future of Imprisonment* (Chicago: University of Chicago Press, 1974), p. 2.

26. Ibid., p. 58. A critique of imprisonment is found in Charles E. Reasons and Russell L. Kaplan, "Tear Down the Walls? Some Functions of Prisons," *Crime and Delinquency* 21 (October 1975): 360–72.

cannot "supply a plausible basis for the advocacy of public policy." Policy based on causal analysis commits the "causal fallacy," which assumes "that no problem is adequately addressed unless its causes are eliminated."[27] Public policy, therefore, should be directed to conditions that can more easily and deliberately be altered. A "policy analysis," as opposed to causal analysis, is accordingly addressed to those conditions that can be manipulated to produce the desired change. That is, for the reduction of crime, the policy analyst focuses on those instruments of control (primarily relating to *deterrence*) that will "at what cost (monetary and nonmonetary), produce how much of a change in the rate of a given crime."[28]

Hence, policy analysis for the new criminal justice is grounded, in both theory and practice policy, in individual utilitarianism. Wilson writes: "The policy analyst is led to assume that the criminal acts *as if* crime were the product of a free choice among competing opportunities and constraints. The radical individualism of Bentham and Beccaria may be scientifically questionable but prudently necessary."[29] The infrastructure of early capitalism is being revitalized to confront the problems of late capitalism.

What are the kinds of policies that follow from this version of reality? The emphasis is on deterrence and incapacitation. For Wilson there is little the police can do in reducing crime, since the police are not the crucial agency in the system. Moreover, rehabilitation does not deter crime. The best that rehabilitation can do is isolate and incapacitate. "Of far greater importance are those agencies

27. Wilson, *Thinking About Crime,* pp. 48–51.
28. Ibid., p. 54. Also John E. Tropman and Karl H. Gohlke, "Cost/Benefit Analysis: Toward Comprehensive Planning in the Criminal Justice System," *Crime and Delinquency* 19 (July 1973): 315–22.
29. Wilson, *Thinking About Crime,* p. 56.

that handle persons once arrested and that determine whether, how soon, and under what conditions they will be returned to the communities from which they came. These agencies are the criminal courts and the correctional institutions."[30] And the function of the courts is not so much to determine guilt or innocence but, in fact, to decide what to do with criminals. Thus, what is needed is "good" sentencing, that is, dispositions that "minimize the chance of a given offender's repeating his crime," considering also the "effect any given sentence will have on actual or potential offenders" and the extent to which the sentence gives "appropriate expression to our moral concern over the offense" and "conform to our standards of humane conduct."[31]

Such sentencing, Wilson continues, should increase the probability of imprisonment, since this appears to deter crime. While severity of penalities "cannot be the norm," certainty of punishment must be. The court system, therefore, is where legal control is best concentrated and dispensed. Nevertheless, Wilson warns, giving some attention to the problem of civil liberties, we in the United States must be willing to "accept both a higher level of crime and disorder and a larger investment in the resources and facilities needed to cope with those who violate the law and, despite our procedural guarantees, are caught by its agents."[32]

The resurgence of interest in crime and punishment is characterized by an even larger problem. In spite of the elaborate legal, philosophical, and behavioralist arguments presented in recent books and articles on crime and punishment, the works lack critical understanding. For it is im-

30. Ibid., p. 163.
31. Ibid., p. 164.
32. Ibid., p. 182.

possible to be convincing when thoughts are grounded entirely within the sensibility of the existing conventional order. What we are given, whether in Wilson's thinking about crime, Morris's proposal for imprisonment, Zimring and Hawkins' scheme for considering deterrence, or in a book such as Jack Gibbs' *Crime, Punishment, and Deterrence,* which in spite of all its theoretical and empirical specification revives the possibility of deterrence as social policy, is a defense of punishment.[33] But more to the point, we are given a defense of punishment that is to be applied within our unique historical context, in the protection of a social order based on late capitalist development. Punishment becomes the solution when our vision is confined within the problem itself. Thus being proposed, and adopted in policy, is the "new justice model" based on punishment, which is expressed in mandatory sentencing, "flat time," and the like.[34] Social theory, if not public policy, should be capable of more than this.

The new justice model is represented in the recent and influential report of the Committee for the Study of Incarceration.[35] The report, *Doing Justice,* combines the work of lawyers, philosophers, historians, and social scientists over a period of several years. Couched in the language of punitive reform, the purpose of the report is to create a

33. Jack P. Gibbs, *Crime, Punishment, and Deterrence* (New York: Elsevier, 1975).
34. See Alan Dershowitz, "Let the Punishment Fit the Crime," *New York Times Magazine,* 28 December 1975, pp. 7, 20–27; "Big Change in Prisons: Punish–Not Reform," *U.S. News & World Report,* 25 August 1975, pp. 21–23; Marcia Chambers, "Radical Changes Urged in Dealing with Youth Crime," *New York Times,* 30 November 1975, p. 1; Edward M. Kennedy, "Punishing the Offenders," *New York Times,* 6 December 1975, p. 29.
35. Andrew Von Hirsch, *Doing Justice: The Choice of Punishments,* Report of the Committee for the Study of Incarceration (New York: Hill & Wang, 1976).

"fairer and less brutal penal system." The criminal sanction of punishment (mainly the length of the prison sentence) is to be limited, but the aim of the report is nevertheless to provide a rationale for punishment. Rather than questioning the nature of the society in the first place, a scheme of punishment is designed to serve the ends of the existing society. In proposing a justice for the present and the future, there is a return to the justice of the past:

> Some of our conclusions may seem old-fashioned. To our surprise, we found ourselves returning to the ideas of such Enlightenment thinkers as Kant and Beccaria–ideas that antedated notions of rehabilitation that emerged in the nineteenth century. We take seriously Kant's view that a person should be punished because he deserves it. We argue, as both Kant and Beccaria did, that severity of punishment should depend chiefly on the seriousness of the crime. We share Beccaria's interest in placing limits on sentencing discretion.[36]

Moreover, punishment is defended on grounds of its deterrent effect and according to the value that those who are defined as criminal *deserve* to be punished. The penalty is a penalty deserved based on the seriousness of the past conduct of the "criminal" and the seriousness of the act in question. Rehabilitation (or any attempt to change behavior) is rejected in favor of a penalty for the behavior. The sentencing system of criminal justice becomes technically rational: "Graded levels of seriousness would be established, and the guidelines would specify which offense categories belong to which seriousness level." [37] Such is the

36. Ibid., p. 6.
37. Ibid., p. 99. Further support for the new justice model is contained in Twentieth Century Task Force on Criminal Sentencing, *Fair and Certain Punishment* (New York: McGraw-Hill, 1976).

nature of reform at the present stage of capitalist development.

When it comes specifically to justice, the revitalization of conventional social theory is restricted to a limited historical version of justice. For Wilson, in his thoughts about the death penalty, justice is reduced to a matter of whether the death penalty subscribes to considerations of "fitness and fairness." [38] Similarly, for Morris in his defense of imprisonment, justice is a matter of "desert," as "the maximum of punishment that the community extracts from the criminal to express the severity of the injury his crime inflicted on the community as a condition of readmitting him to society." [39] Morris, in drawing from John Rawls' rationalistic treatise on justice (a variant within the utilitarian tradition), determines the extent of criminal punishment and imprisonment according to what is "deserved" by the crime of the offender.

All these writings subscribe to a combination of two unique notions of justice. They conceive of justice as protecting acknowledged "rights" within the current order and as distributing punishment according to desert. The new justice model dispenses justice (i.e., punishment) for the purpose of preserving the capitalist social order and according to what the offender deserves in the pursual of rational action. This notion of justice is appropriate for the capitalist order; it assumes a hierarchy of rights and competitive social relations.

There is, however, an alternative to the capitalist notions of justice. In sharp contrast to the new justice model (which is actually a mixture of old justice) is the idea of justice as distribution according to *need*. David Miller, in his recent

38. Wilson, *Thinking About Crime,* p. 184.
39. Morris, *Future of Imprisonment,* p. 74.

article "The Ideological Backgrounds to Conceptions of Social Justice," suggests that this latter form of justice is appropriate for a society that is based on cooperative social relations, a communal society, and a developing socialist society.[40] It assumes that human beings behave (or are capable of behaving) cooperatively and altruistically without the use of financial rewards or penal sanctions. While not likely to be found in capitalist societies, this notion of justice nevertheless has its own tradition. It is found in early and latter-day communal and religious movements, with basic elements present in socialist countries today.

As capitalist society continues to develop its own contradictions and crises, the contrasts between divergent conceptions of justice become evident. What we are witnessing in the recent theories and practices of criminal justice is an attempt to reestablish a justice appropriate to a former age, a justice that ignores historical development but one that would seemingly preserve the contemporary capitalist order.

However, class struggle today is also a struggle for a new justice. Beyond the conventional notions of crime and punishment is the creation of a new social order. In question is not merely the extent of justice but what kind and under what conditions. Now we are beginning to attend to a socialist sense of justice.

CRITIQUE OF JUSTICE

As the struggle continues we begin to ask whether "justice" is the appropriate way of visioning and realizing a better world. Is there another way of proceeding? The classic

40. David Miller, "The Ideological Backgrounds to Conceptions of Social Justice," *Political Studies* 22 (December 1974): 387–99.

dichotomy about the meaning of justice dominates contemporary social science and ethical discourse. That dichotomy is found in the debate between Socrates and Thrasymachus that Plato chronicles in the first book of the *Republic*.[41] When the question "What is justice?" is posed, Thrasymachus responds that "justice is the interest of the stronger," elaborating that what is regarded as just in a society is determined by the ruling elite acting in its own interest. Later Socrates gives his formulation of justice as "everyone having and doing what is appropriate to him," that is, people trying to do the right thing.

Obviously, Thrasymachus and Socrates are talking about two different problems. While Thrasymachus is giving us a factual description of how justice actually operates, Socrates is telling us about what people think they are doing when they attend to that which is called "justice."[42] There is justice as an ideal of goodness and justice in practice in everyday life. And justice as officially practiced in contemporary society is the idealized and practical justice of the capitalist class, as administered through the legal system of the capitalist state. The question for us, then, given a Marxist understanding of the class and state character of justice, represented in the Thrasymachus position, is whether the most productive way of talking about truth, beauty, and goodness, about a socialist vision, is in terms of "justice." Or, in other words, is there a Marxist morality? More to the point, what is the Marxist way of attending to correct action and the creation of a better life? Can we conduct our lives in a way that surpasses the language of justice?

At the present stage of our development, the concept of

41. This debate is discussed in Hanna Fenichel Pitkin, *Wittgenstein and Justice* (Berkeley: University of California Press, 1972), pp. 169–92.
42. Ibid., p. 170.

justice serves the larger purpose of providing a standard by which we judge concrete actions. We critically understand the actions of the capitalist state, including the administration of criminal justice, because we have an idea of how things could be. Critical thought and related actions are made possible because we transcend the conventional ideology of capitalism. Because we have a notion of something else, a socialist life, we refuse to accept capitalist justice in both theory and practice. Critical thought, as Hannah Arendt has noted, allows us to interrupt all ordinary activity, entering into a different existence: "Thinking, the quest for meaning–rather than the scientist's thirst for knowledge for its own sake–can be felt to be 'unnatural,' as though men, when they begin to think, engage in some activity contrary to the human condition." [43] In talking and thinking about how things *could be,* we engage in thoughts and actions that are directed to the realization of a different life. Arendt adds that only with the desiring love of wisdom, beauty, and the like are we prepared with a kind of life that promotes a moral existence. Only when we are filled with what Socrates called *eros,* a love that desires what is not, do we attempt to find what is good. Thinking and acting critically is thus political. In collective effort, we change our form of life and alter the mode of social existence.

If any body of thought has a notion of truth and beauty, of how things could be, it is that of Marxism. In fact, Marxism is the one philosophy of our time that takes as its primary focus the oppression of capitalist society. It is the one analysis that is historically specific and locates contemporary problems in the existing political economy. Marxist

43. Hannah Arendt, "Thinking and Moral Considerations," *Social Research* 38 (Autumn 1971): 424.

theory provides, most importantly, a form of thought that allows us to transcend in theory and practice the oppression of the capitalist order.

Yet the question remains: Is "justice" necessary in Marxist theory and practice? Recent discussions have shown that Marx himself avoided the use of a justice terminology.[44] Marx steered away from justice-talk because he regarded it as "ideological twaddle," detracting from a critical analysis of the capitalist system as a whole. Both Marx and Engels were in fact highly critical of the use of the justice notion, used as a way of mystifying the actual operation of capitalism. At the same time, they found a way critically to understand capitalism that carried with it a condemnation that goes far beyond any notion of justice. Thus, Marxist analysis moves us beyond the classic dichotomy of the justice debate, providing us as well with a deeper understanding of the capitalist system, a vision of a different world, and a political life in struggling for that society.

The problem with the concept of justice, according to Marx and Engels, is that it is fundamentally a juridical or legal concept. As such, the concept of justice is restricted to rational standards by which laws, social institutions, and human actions are judged.[45] Moreover, this restricted analysis fails to grasp the material conditions, the real basis of society. Human life is to be understood in terms of the productive forces and relations of society, with the state as an expression of the prevailing mode of production.[46] To

44. William Leon McBride, "The Concept of Justice in Marx, Engels, and Others," *Ethics* 85 (April 1975): 204–18; Allen W. Wood, "The Marxian Critique of Justice," *Philosophy and Public Affairs* 1 (Spring 1972): 244–82.
45. Wood, "Marxian Critique of Justice," p. 246.
46. Karl Marx, *A Contribution to the Critique of Political Economy*, ed. M. Dobb (New York: International Publishers, 1970), pp. 19–23.

focus on the juridical nature of social reality is to misunderstand the material basis of reality. An analysis limited to questions of justice systematically excludes the important questions about capitalist society.

The critique of capitalism for Marx is provided in the very form of the capitalist system. Capitalism rests on the appropriation of labor power from the working class. Capital is accumulated by the capitalist class in the course of underpaying the workers for products made by their own labor. The capitalist mode of production depends on "surplus value," on unpaid labor. Capitalism itself is a system of exploitation. The servitude of the wage laborer to capital is essential to the capitalist mode of production.

When the system itself is oppressive, to call it "unjust" is to miss its larger, more pervasive, design. A justice terminology limits our understanding as well as restricts our actions. "Marx's call to the revolutionary overthrow of capitalist production therefore is not, and cannot be, founded on claims that capitalism is unjust. Marx in fact regarded all attempts to base revolutionary practice on juridical notions as an 'ideological shuffle,' and he dismissed the use of terms like 'equal right' and 'just distribution' in the working-class movement as 'outdated verbal trivia.' "[47] Marx's condemnation of capitalism and the need for revolutionary action is based on the innate character of capitalism, on an understanding of capitalism as a whole and on its position in human history.

We have thus moved out of the classical dichotomy between value and fact. "Justice" embodies the classical dichotomy, representing a standard for measuring actual occurrences. In developing a Marxist analysis, however, value and fact are integrated into a comprehensive scheme.

47. Wood, "Marxian Critique of Justice," pp. 271–72.

Values are always attached to what we take to be facts, and facts cannot exist apart from values. As Bertell Ollman observes in his discussion of Marx's method:

> It is not simply that the "facts" affect our "values," and our "values" affect what we take to be the "facts"–both respectably common sense positions–but that, in any given case, each includes the other and is part of what is meant by the other's concept. In these circumstances, to try to split their union into logically distinct halves is to distort their real character.[48]

In a Marxist analysis, the description of social reality is at the same time an evaluation. Nothing is "morally neutral" in such an understanding. The description contains within itself its own condemnation and, moreover, a call to do something about the condition. The critique is at once a description of the condition and the possibility for transforming it. All things are in relation to one another–are one in the other.

The notion of justice will not disappear immediately from philosophical and everyday discourse. Language does not change outside of social conditions. Language reform is not the solution: "Marx and Engels were not interested in posing as mere language reformers; they anticipated the withering away of justice-talk as only one by-product of a possible future fundamental social change from capitalism to socialism." [49] As Marxists, we live simultaneously in the past, present, and future. The dialectic is one of anticipating the future, with new patterns of life and language, but

48. Bertell Ollman, *Alienation: Marx's Conception of Man in Capitalist Society* (New York: Cambridge University Press, 1971), p. 48.
49. McBride, "Concept of Justice in Marx, Engels, and Others," p. 215.

also immersed in the everyday reality of the present. That terms such as "justice," or perhaps "social justice," may be used today is an expression of this dialectic. The transition to socialism is the path we are now beginning. As we reach the first stages of socialism, with unforseen horizons beyond, we will begin to create the correct forms.

2

CRIME AND THE DEVELOPMENT OF CAPITALISM

Marxist analysis has moved us to new questions about the nature of crime in capitalist society. Heretofore our understanding was limited by a narrow set of problems, confined by a bourgeois mentality that promoted the existing order. We have since been forced to reexamine our efforts in the study of crime. In the process we are gaining a new understanding of crime.

MARXIST ANALYSIS OF CRIME

A Marxist analysis of crime begins with the recognition that crime is basically a material problem. In fact, the crucial phenomenon to be considered is not crime per se, but the historical development and operation of the capitalist economy.[1] Any study of crime involves an investigation of such natural products and contradictions of capitalism as poverty, inequality, unemployment, and the economic crisis of the capitalist state. Ultimately, however, to understand crime we must understand the development of the political economy of capitalist society.

The necessary condition for any society, according to the materialist method and conception of reality, is that its members produce their material means of subsistence. Social production is therefore the primary process of all social life. Moreover, in the social production of our existence we enter into relations that are appropriate to the existing forces of production.[2] It is this "economic" structure that provides the foundation for all social and political institutions, for everyday life, and for social consciousness. Our analysis thus begins with the *material conditions* of social life.

The *dialectical method* allows us to comprehend the world as a complex of processes, in which all things go through a continuous process of coming into being and passing away. All things are studied in the context of their historical development. Dialectical materialism allows us to learn about things as they are in their actual interconnection, contradiction, and movement. In dialectical analysis we critically understand our past, informing our analysis with the possibilities for our future.

A Marxist analysis shares in the larger *socialist struggle*. There is the commitment to eliminating exploitation and oppression. Being on the side of the oppressed, only those

1. Paul Q. Hirst, "Marx and Engels on Law, Crime and Morality," *Economy and Society* 1 (February 1972): 28–56.
2. Karl Marx, *A Contribution to the Critique of Political Economy*, ed. M. Dobb (New York: International Publishers, 1970), pp. 20–21.

ideas are advanced that will aid in transforming the capitalist system. The objective of the Marxist analysis is change—revolutionary change. The purpose of our intellectual labors is to assist in providing knowledge and consciousness for building a socialist society. Theories and strategies are developed to increase conscious class struggle; ideas for an alternative to capitalist society are formulated; and strategies for achieving the socialist alternative are proposed. In the course of intellectual-political work we engage in the activities and actions that will advance the socialist struggle.

With these notions of a Marxist analysis—encompassing a dialectical-historical analysis of the material conditions of capitalist society in relation to socialist revolution—we begin to formulate the significant substantive questions about crime. In recent years, as socialists have turned their attention to the study of crime, the outline for these questions has become evident. At this stage in our intellectual development the important questions revolve around *the meaning of crime in capitalist society*. Furthermore, there is the realization that the meaning of crime changes in the course of the development of capitalism.

The basic problem in any study of the meaning of crime is that of integrating the two sides of the crime phenomenon: placing into a single framework (1) the defining of behavior as criminal (i.e., *crime control*) and (2) the behavior of those who are defined as criminal (i.e., *criminality*). Thus far, the analysis of crime has focused on one side or the other, failing to integrate the two interrelated processes into one scheme. In pursuing a Marxist analysis, however, the problem of the dual nature of the concept of crime is solved by *giving primacy to the underlying political economy*.

The basic question in the Marxist analysis of crime is thus formulated: What is the meaning of crime in the develop-

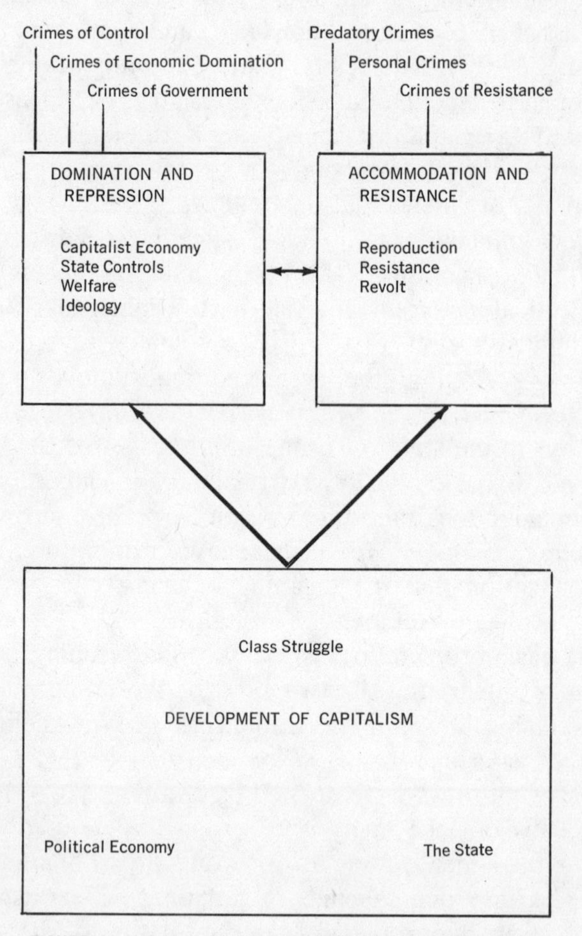

FIGURE 1. CRIME AND THE DEVELOPMENT OF CAPITALISM.

ment of capitalism? In approaching this question, we must give attention to several interrelated processes: (1) the development of capitalist political economy, including the nature of the forces and relations of production, the formulation of the capitalist state, and the class struggle between those who do and those who do not own and control the means of production; (2) the systems of domination and repression that are established in the development of capitalism, operating for the benefit of the capitalist class and secured by the capitalist state; (3) the forms of accommodation and resistance to the conditions of capitalism, by all people oppressed by capitalism, especially the working class; and (4) the relation of the dialectics of domination and accommodation to patterns of crime in capitalist society, producing the crimes of domination and the crimes of accommodation. As indicated in figure 1, all these processes are dialectically related to the developing political economy. Crime is to be understood in terms of the development of capitalism.

DEVELOPMENT OF CAPITALIST ECONOMY

Crime, as noted, is a manifestation of the material conditions of society. The failure of conventional criminology is to ignore, by design, the material conditions of capitalism. Since the phenomena of crime are products of the substructure—are themselves part of the superstructure—any explanation of crime in terms of other elements of the superstructure is no explanation at all. Our need is to develop a general materialist framework for understanding crime, beginning with the underlying historical processes of social existence.

Production, as the necessary requirement of existence,

produces its own forces and relations of social and economic life. The material factors (such as resources and technology) and personal factors (most importantly the workers) present at any given time form the productive *forces* of society. In the process of production, people form definite relations with one another. These *relations* of production, in reference to the forces of production, constitute the particular *mode* of production of any society at any given time. The economic mode of production furnishes society with its substructure, on which the social and political institutions (including crime control) and supporting ideologies are built.

Once the outlines of *political economy* (the productive forces, the relations of production, and the superstructure) have been indicated, the *class structure* and its dynamics can be recognized. A class society arises when the system of production is owned by one segment of the society to the exclusion of another. All production requires ownership of some kind; but in some systems of production ownership is private rather than social or collective. In these economies social relations are dependent on relations of domination and subjection. Marxist economists thus observe: "Relations of domination and subjection are based on private ownership of the means of production and express the exploitation of man by man under the slave-owning, feudal and capitalist systems. Relations of friendly co-operation and mutual assistance between working people free of exploitation are typical of socialist society. They are based on the public ownership of the means of production, which cut out exploitation." [3]

All social life in capitalist society, including everything

3. L. Afanasyev et al., *The Political Economy of Capitalism* (Moscow: Progress Publishers, 1974), p. 12.

associated with crime, therefore, must be understood in terms of the economic conditions of production and the struggle between classes produced by these conditions. In other words, in capitalist society the life and behavior of any group in the society, or any individual group member, can be understood only in terms of the conflict that characterizes class relations, which in turn is produced by the capitalist system of production. The life and behavior of one class are seen in relation to that of the other. As E. P. Thompson observes, an analysis of class entails the notion of the historical *relationship* of classes:

> Like any other relationship, it is a fluency which evades analysis if we attempt to stop it dead at any given moment and anatomise its structure. The finest-meshed sociological net cannot give us a pure specimen of class, any more than it can give us one of deference or of love. The relationship must always be embodied in real people in a real context. Moreover, we cannot have two distinct classes, each with an independent being, and then bring them *into* relationship with each other. We cannot have love without lovers, nor deference without squires and laborers. And class happens when some men, as a result of common experiences (inherited or shared), feel and articulate the identity of their interests as between themselves, and as against other men whose interests are different from (and usually opposed to) theirs. The class experience is largely determined by the productive relations into which men are born–or enter involuntarily.[4]

Hence, class in capitalist society is analyzed in reference to the relationship to the process of production and according to the relationship to other classes in the society.

Moreover, the problematics of *labor* (as the foremost

4. E. P. Thompson, *The Making of the English Working Class* (New York: Random House, 1963), p. 9.

human activity) characterize the nature and specific relationship of the classes. For the capitalist system to operate and survive, the capitalist class must exploit the labor (appropriate the *surplus labor*) of the working class. As Maurice Dobb notes,

> the relationship from which in one case a common interest in preserving and extending a particular economic system and in the other case an antagonism of interest on this issue can alone derive must be a relationship with a particular mode of extracting and distributing the fruits of surplus labour, over and above the labour which goes to supply the consumption of the actual producer. Since this surplus labor constitutes its life-blood, any ruling class will of necessity treat its particular relationship to the labour-process as crucial to its own survival; and any rising class that aspires to live without labour is bound to regard its own future career, prosperity and influence as dependent on the acquisition of some claim upon the surplus labour of others.[5]

The capitalist class survives by appropriating the surplus labor of the working class, and the working class as an exploited class exists as long as surplus labor is required in the productive process: each class depends on the other for its character and existence.

The amount of labor appropriated, the techniques of labor exploitation, the conditions of working-class life, and the level of working-class consciousness have all been an integral part of the historical development of capitalism.[6] In like manner, the degree of antagonism and conflict be-

5. Maurice Dobb, *Studies in the Development of Capitalism* (New York: International Publishers, 1963), p. 15.
6. Jurgen Kuczynski, *The Rise of the Working Class* (New York: McGraw-Hill, 1967).

tween classes has varied at different stages in the development. Nevertheless, it is the basic contradiction between classes, generalized as class conflict, that typifies the development of capitalism. Class conflict permeates the whole of capitalist development, represented in the contradiction between those who own property and those who do not, and by those who oppress and those who are oppressed.[7] All past history, that involving the development of capitalism, is the history of class struggle.

Capitalism as a system of production based on the exploitation by the ruling capitalist class that owns and controls the means of production is thus a dynamic system that goes through its own stages of development. In fact, capitalism is constantly transforming its own forces and relations of production. As a result, the whole of capitalist society is constantly being altered–within the basic framework of capitalist political economy.

The Marxian view stresses the qualitative changes in social organization and social relations as well as (or in relation to) the quantitative changes in the economic system.[8] Capitalism transforms itself, affecting the social existence of all who live under it. This is the basic dynamic of capitalist development, an interdependence between production, the relations of production, and the social superstructure of institutions and ideas. "For it is a requirement of all social production that the relations which people enter into in carrying on production must be suitable to the type of production they are carrying on. Hence, it is a general law of economic development that the relations of

7. Robert Heiss, *Engels, Kierkegaard, and Marx* (New York: Dell, 1975), p. 390.
8. Paul M. Sweezy, *The Theory of Capitalist Development* (New York: Monthly Review Press, 1968), pp. 92–95.

production must necessarily be adapted to the character of the forces of production." [9]

As the preceding discussion indicates, analysis of the meaning of crime in the development of capitalism necessarily involves an investigation of the relation between the concrete stage of capitalist development and of the social relations that correspond to that stage of development. This is not to argue that the superstructure of social relations and culture is an automatic (directly determined) product of the economic substructure. After all, people may enter into relations of production in various ways in order to employ the given forces of production; and it is on the basis of these relations that they create further institutions and ideas. Since human social existence is in part a product of conscious activity and struggle, conscious life must be part of any analysis. Maurice Cornforth, in a discussion of historical materialism, puts it well:

> But ideas and institutions are not the automatic products of a given economic and class structure, but products of people's conscious activities and struggles. To explain the superstructure, these activities and struggles must be studied concretely, in their actual complex development. Therefore it is certainly not Marxism, just as it is certainly not science, to attempt to conclude from the specification of certain economic conditions what the form of the superstructure arising on that basis is going to be, or to deduce every detailed characteristic of the superstructure from some corresponding feature of the basis. On the contrary, we need to study how the superstructure actually develops in each society and in each epoch, by investigating the facts about that society and that epoch.[10]

9. Maurice Cornforth, *Historical Materialism* (New York: International Publishers, 1962), p. 59.
10. Ibid., p. 91.

Such is the basic task in our study of the meaning of crime in the development of capitalism.

In addition, the more developed the productive forces under capitalism, the greater the discrepancy between the productive forces and the capitalist relations of production. Capitalist development, with economic expansion being fundamental to capitalist economic development, exacerbates rather than mitigates the contradictions of capitalism.[11] Workers are further exploited, conditions of existence worsen, while the contradictions of capitalism increase. Capitalist development, in other words, and from another vantage point, creates the conditions for the transformation and abolition of capitalism, brought about in actuality by class struggle.

The history of capitalism can thus be traced according to the nature of capitalist development. The main contradictions of capitalism are concretely formed and manifested in each stage of development. The forms and intensity of exploitation are documented and understood in respect to the particular character of capitalism at each development stage. How crime–control of crime and criminality–plays its part in each stage of capitalist development is our concern in any investigation of the meaning of crime.

The periods of capitalist development, for our purposes, differ according to the ways in which surplus labor is appropriated. Capitalism, as distinct from other modes of production, has gone through periods that utilize various methods of production and create social relations in association with these productive forms. Each new development in capitalism, conditioned by the preceding historical processes, brings about its own particular forms of capi-

11. Erik Ohlin Wright, "Alternative Perspectives in the Marxist Theory of Accumulation and Crisis," *Insurgent Sociologist* 6 (Fall 1975): 5–39.

talist economy and social reality–and related problems of human existence.

Any investigation of the meaning (and changing meanings) of crime in America, therefore, requires a delineation of the periods of economic development in the United States. A few attempts at such delineation already exist, but for other than the study of crime. For example, Douglas Dowd in his book *The Twisted Dream* notes briefly three different periods of American development, with particular reference to the role of the state in American economic life: (1) American mercantilism, up to Jackson's Presidency; (2) laissez-faire capitalism, coming to a climax in the decades after the Civil War; and (3) maturing industrial capitalism, up to the present.[12] Similarly, in another treatment, William A. Williams in his book *The Contours of American History* arranges American history according to the following periods: (1) the age of mercantilism, 1740–1828; (2) the age of laissez nous faire, 1819–96; and (3) the age of corporate capitalism, 1882 to the present.[13] To this scheme, others add that American capitalism is now in the stage of either "monopoly capital" or "finance capital."[14]

It is debatable, nevertheless, in our study of crime in the United States, whether America was capitalist from

12. Douglas F. Dowd, *The Twisted Dream: Capitalist Development in the United States Since 1776* (Cambridge, Mass.: Winthrop, 1974), pp. 42–48.
13. William Appleman Williams, *The Contours of American History* (New York: World, 1961).
14. Paul A. Baran and Paul M. Sweezy, *Monopoly Capital: An Essay on the American Economic and Social Order* (New York: Monthly Review Press, 1966). Robert Fitch and Mary Oppenheimer, "Who Rules the Corporations," *Socialist Revolution,* no. 4 (July–August 1970): 73–107; no. 5 (September–October 1970): 61–114; no. 6 (November–December 1970): 33–94.

the beginning, with capitalism merely imported from the Old to the New World. Or whether, as James O'Connor has recently argued, capitalist development has occurred in only fairly recent times.[15] For the first hundred years of nationhood the United States resisted large-scale capitalist production. Independent commodity production predominated; farmers, artisans, small manufacturers and other petty producers were the mainstay of the economy. Only as northern capitalists acquired land from the farmers (thus appropriating their labor power) and as immigrant labor power was imported from Europe did capitalism finally emerge in the United States. American capitalism emerged when capitalists won the battle as to who was to control labor power. Surplus labor was now in the hands of a capitalist ruling class. Workers could be exploited.

For certain, we are today in a stage of late, advanced capitalism in the United States. The current meaning of crime in America can be understood only in relation to the character of capitalism in the present era. Similarly, the meanings of crime at various times in the past have to be understood according to the particular stage of development. Only in the investigation of crime in the development of capitalism do we truly understand the meaning of crime. Concrete research will provide us with knowledge about the role of crime in the development of capitalism.

DOMINATION AND REPRESSION

The capitalist system must be continuously reproduced. This is accomplished in a variety of ways, ranging from the establishment of ideological hegemony to the further ex-

15. James O'Connor, "The Twisted Dream," *Monthly Review* 26 (March 1975): 46–53.

ploitation of labor, from the creation of public policy to the coercive repression of the population. Most explicitly, the *state* secures the capitalist order. Through various schemes and mechanisms, then, the capitalist class is able to dominate. And in the course of this domination, crimes are carried out. These crimes, committed by the capitalist class, the state, and the agents of the capitalist class and state, are the crimes of domination.

Historically the capitalist state is a product of a political economy that depends on a division of classes. With the development of an economy based on the exploitation of one class by another, there was the need for a political form that would perpetuate that kind of order. With the development of capitalism, with class divisions and class struggle, the state became necessary. A new stage of development, Frederick Engels observes, called for the creation of the state:

> Only one thing was wanting: an institution which not only secured the newly acquired riches of individuals against the communistic traditions of the gentile order, which not only sanctified the private property formerly so little valued, and declared this sanctification to be the highest purpose of all human society; but an institution which set the seal of general social recognition on each new method of acquiring property and thus amassing wealth at continually increased speed; an institution which perpetuated, not only this growing cleavage of society into classes, but also the right of the possessing class to exploit the non-possessing, and the rule of the former over the latter.
>
> And this institution came. The state was invented.[16]

The state thus arose to protect and promote the interests of the dominant class, the class that owns and controls

16. Frederick Engels, *The Origin of the Family, Private Property, and the State* (New York: International Publishers, 1942), p. 97.

the means of production. The state exists as a devic controlling the exploited class, the class that labors, for the benefit of the ruling class. Modern civilization, as epitomized in capitalist societies, is founded on the exploitation of one class by another. Moreover, the capitalist state is oppressive not only because it supports the interests of the dominant class but also because it is responsible for the design of the whole system within which the capitalist ruling class dominates and the working class is dominated.[17] The capitalist system of production and exploitation is secured and reproduced by the capitalist state.

The coercive force of the state, embodied in law and legal repression, is the traditional means of maintaining the social and economic order. Contrary to conventional wisdom, law instead of representing community custom is an instrument of the state that serves the interests of the developing capitalist ruling class. Law emerged with the rise of capitalism, as Stanley Diamond writes: "Law arises in the breach of a prior customary order and increases in force with the conflicts that divide political societies internally and among themselves. Law *and* order is the historical illusion; law versus order is the historical reality."[18] Law and legal repression are, and continue to serve as, the means of enforcing the interests of the dominant class in the capitalist state.

Through the legal system, then, the state forcefully protects its interests and those of the capitalist ruling class. Crime control becomes the coercive means of checking threats to the existing social and economic order, threats

17. David A. Gold, Clarence Y. H. Lo, and Erik Olin Wright, "Recent Developments in Marxist Theories of the State," *Monthly Review* 27 (November 1975): 36–51.
18. Stanley Diamond, "The Rule of Law Versus the Order of Custom," *Social Research* 38 (Spring 1971): 71.

that result from a system of oppression and exploitation. As a means of controlling the behavior of the exploited population, crime control is accomplished by a variety of methods, strategies, and institutions.[19] The state, especially through its legislative bodies, establishes official policies of crime control. The administrative branch of the state establishes and enforces crime-control policies, usually setting the design for the whole nation. Specific agencies of law enforcement, such as the Federal Bureau of Investigation and the recent Law Enforcement Assistance Administration, determine the nature of crime control. And the state is able through its Department of Justice officially to repress the "dangerous" and "subversive" elements of the population. Altogether, these state institutions attempt to rationalize the legal system by employing the advanced methods of science and technology. And whenever any changes are to be attempted to reduce the incidence of crime, rehabilitation of the individual or reform within the existing institutions is suggested.[20] Drastically to alter the society and the crime-control establishment would be to alter beyond recognition the capitalist system.

Yet the coercive force of the state is but one means of maintaining the social and economic order. A more subtle reproductive mechanism of capitalist society is the perpetuation of the capitalist conception of reality, a nonviolent but equally repressive means of domination. As Alan Wolfe has shown, in the manipulation of consciousness the existing order is legitimated and secured:

> The most important reproductive mechanism which does not involve the use of state violence is consciousness-manipula-

19. See Richard Quinney, *Critique of Legal Order: Crime Control in Capitalist Society* (Boston: Little, Brown, 1974), pp. 95–135.
20. Alexander Liazos, "Class Oppression: The Functions of Juvenile Justice," *Insurgent Sociologist* 5 (Fall 1974): 2–24.

tion. The liberal state has an enormous amount of violence at its disposal, but it is often reluctant to use it. Violence may breed counter-violence, leading to instability. It may be far better to manipulate consciousness to such an extent that most people would never think of engaging in the kinds of action which could be repressed. The most perfectly repressive (though not violently so) capitalist system, in other words, would not be a police state, but the complete opposite, one in which there were no police because there was nothing to police, everyone having accepted the legitimacy of that society and all its daily consequences.[21]

Those who rule in capitalist society—with the assistance of the state—not only accumulate capital at the expense of those who work but impose their ideology as well. Oppression and exploitation are legitimized by the expropriation of consciousness; since labor is expropriated, consciousness must also be expropriated.[22] In fact, *legitimacy* of the capitalist order is maintained by controlling the consciousness of the population. A capitalist hegemony is established.

Thus, through its various reproductive mechanisms capitalism is able to maximize the possibility of control over the citizens of the state. Ranging from control of production and distribution to manipulation of the mind, capitalism operates according to its own form of dictatorship. André Gorz writes:

> The dictatorship of capital is exercised not only on the production and distribution of wealth, but with equal force on the manner of producing, on the model of consumption, and on the manner of consuming, the manner of working, think-

21. Alan Wolfe, "Political Repression and the Liberal State," *Monthly Review* 23 (December 1971): 20.
22. Alan Wolfe, "New Directions in the Marxist Theory of Politics," *Politics and Society* 4 (Winter 1974): 155–57.

> ing, living. As much as over the workers, the factories, and the state, this dictatorship rules over the society's vision of the future, its ideology, its priorities and goals, over the way in which people experience and learn about themselves, their potentials, their relations with other people and with the rest of the world. This dictatorship is economic, political, cultural and pyschological at the same time: it is total.[23]

Moreover, a society that depends on surplus labor for its existence must not only control that situation but also must cope with the problems that economic system naturally creates. The capitalist state must therefore provide "social services" in the form of education, health, welfare, and rehabilitation programs of various kinds, to deal with the problems that could otherwise be dealt with only by changing the capitalist system. These state services function as a repressive means of securing the capitalist order.

Capitalism systematically generates a *surplus population,* an unemployed sector of the working class either dependent on fluctuations in the economy or made obsolete by new technology. With the growth of the surplus population, pressures build up for the growth of the welfare system. The function of expanding welfare, with its host of services, is to control the surplus population politically. Moreover, O'Connor observes, "Unable to gain employment in the monopoly industries by offering their laborpower at lower than going wage rates (and victimized by sexism and racism), and unemployed, underemployed, or employed at low wages in competitive industries, the surplus population increasingly becomes dependent on the state." [24] An unsteady alliance is thus formed between the

23. André Gorz, *Strategy for Labor: A Radical Proposal,* tr. Martin A. Nicolaus and Victoria Ortiz (Boston: Beacon Press, 1967), pp. 131–32.
24. James O'Connor, *The Fiscal Crisis of the State* (New York: St. Martin's Press, 1973), p. 161.

causalties it naturally produces. Only a new economic order could replace the need for a welfare state.

Repression through welfare is in part the history of capitalism. The kinds of services have varied with the development of economic conditions. In the same way, relief policies have varied according to specific tensions produced by unemployment and subsequent threats of disorder. As Frances Fox Piven and Richard A. Cloward write in their study of the modern welfare system:

> Relief arrangements are ancillary to economic arrangements. Their chief function is to regulate labor, and they do that in two general ways. First, when mass unemployment leads to outbreaks of turmoil, relief programs are ordinarily initiated or expanded to absorb and control enough of the unemployed to restore order; then, as turbulence subsides, the relief system contracts, expelling those who are needed to populate the labor market. Relief also performs a labor-regulating function in this shrunken state, however. Some of the aged, the disabled, the insane, and others who are of no use as workers are left on the relief rolls, and their treatment is so degrading and punitive as to instill in the laboring masses a fear of the fate that awaits them should they relax into beggary and pauperism. To demean and punish those who do not work is to exalt by contrast even the meanest labor at the meanest wages. These regulative functions of relief, and their periodic expansion and contraction, are made necessary by several strains toward instability inherent in capitalist economies.[25]

Control through welfare can never be a permanent solution for a system based on appropriation of labor. As with all the forms of control and manipulation in capitalist society,

25. Frances Fox Piven and Richard A. Cloward, *Regulating the Poor: The Functions of Public Welfare* (New York: Random House, 1971), pp. 3–4.

welfare cannot completely counter the basic contradictions of a capitalist political economy.

Although the capitalist state creates and manages the institutions of control (employing physical force *and* manipulation of consciousness), the basic contradictions of the capitalist order are such that this control is not absolute and, in the long run, is subject to defeat. Because of the contradictions of capitalism, the capitalist state is more weak than strong.[26] Eventually the capitalist state loses its legitimacy, no longer being able to perpetuate the ideology that capital accumulation for capitalists (at the expense of workers) is good for the nation or for human interests. The ability of the capitalist economic order to exist according to its own interests is eventually weakened.[27] The problem becomes especially acute in periods of economic crisis, periods that are unavoidable under capitalism.

In the course of reproducing the capitalist system crimes are committed. It is a contradiction of capitalism that some of its laws must be violated in order to secure the existing system.[28] The contradictions of capitalism produce their own sources of crime. Not only are these contradictions heightened during times of crisis, making for increased crimes of domination, but the nature of these crimes changes with the further development of capitalism.

The crimes of domination most characteristic of capi-

26. Wolfe, "New Directions in the Marxist Theory of Politics," p. 155.
27. See Stanley Aronowitz, "Law, Breakdown of Order, and Revolution," in *Law Against the People: Essays to Demystify Law, Order and the Courts,* ed. Robert Lefcourt (New York: Random House, 1971), pp. 150–82; and John H. Schaar, "Legitimacy in the Modern State," in *Power and Community: Dissenting Essays in Political Science,* ed. Philip Green and Sanford Levinson (New York: Random House, 1970), pp. 276–327.
28. See Richard Quinney, *Criminology: Analysis and Critique of Crime in America* (Boston: Little, Brown, 1975), pp. 131–61.

talist domination are those that occur in the course of state control. These are the *crimes of control.* They include the felonies and misdemeanors that law-enforcement agents, especially the police, carry out in the name of the law, usually against persons accused of other violations. Violence and brutality have become a recognized part of police work. In addition to these crimes of control, there are the crimes of more subtle nature in which agents of the law violate the civil liberties of citizens, as in the various forms of surveillance, the use of provocateurs, and the illegal denial of due process.

Then there are the *crimes of government,* committed by the elected and appointed officials of the capitalist state. The Watergate crimes, carried out to perpetuate a particular governmental administration, are the most publicized instances of these crimes. There are also those offenses committed by the government against persons and groups who would seemingly threaten national security. Included here are the crimes of warfare and the political assassination of foreign and domestic leaders.

Crimes of domination also consist of those crimes that occur in the capitalist class for the purpose of securing the existing economic order. These *crimes of economic domination* include the crimes committed by corporations, ranging from price fixing to pollution of the environment in order to protect and further capital accumulation. Also included are the economic crimes of individual businessmen and professionals. In addition, the crimes of the capitalist class and the capitalist state are joined in organized crime. The more conventional criminal operations of organized crime are linked to the state in the present stage of capitalist development. The operations of organized crime and the criminal operations of the state are united in the attempt to assure the survival of the capitalist system.

Finally, many *social injuries* are committed by the capitalist class and the capitalist state that are not usually defined as criminal in the legal codes of the state.[29] These systematic actions, involving the denial of basic human rights (resulting in sexism, racism, and economic exploitation) are an integral part of capitalism and are important to its survival.

Underlying all the capitalist crimes is the appropriation of the surplus value created by labor. The working class has the right to possess the whole of this value. The worker creates a value several times greater than the labor power purchased by the capitalist. The excess value created by the worker over and above the value of labor power is the surplus value which is appropriated by the capitalist. Surplus value, as exploitation, is essential to capitalism, being the source of accumulation of capital and expansion of production.

Domination and repression are a basic part of class struggle in the development of capitalism. The capitalist class and state protect and promote the capitalist order by controlling those who do not own the means of production. The labor supply and the conditions for labor must be secured. Crime control and the crimes of domination are thus necessary features and the natural products of capitalist political economy.

ACCOMMODATION AND RESISTANCE

The contradictions of developing capitalism increase the level of class struggle and thereby increase (1) the need

29. Tony Platt, "Prospects for a Radical Criminology in the United States," *Crime and Social Justice* 1 (Spring–Summer, 1974): 2–10; Herman and Julia Schwendinger, "Defenders of Order or Guardians of Human Rights?" *Issues in Criminology* 5 (Summer 1970): 123–57.

to dominate by the capitalist class and (2) the need to accommodate and resist by the classes that are exploited by capitalism, particularly the working class. Most of the behavior in response to domination, including the actions of the oppressed that are defined as criminal by the capitalist class, is a product of the capitalist system of production. In the course of capitalist appropriation of labor, for the accumulation of capital, conditions are established which call for behaviors that may be defined as criminal by the capitalist state. These behaviors become eligible for crime control when they disturb or threaten in some way the capitalist order.[30]

Hence, the class that does not own or control the means of production must adapt to the conditions of capitalism. Accommodation and resistance to the conditions of capitalism are basic to the class struggle. The argument here is that action by people who do not own and control the means of production, those who are exploited and oppressed, is largely an accommodation or resistance to the conditions produced by capitalist production. Thus, criminality among the oppressed classes is action (conscious or otherwise) in relation to the capitalist order of exploitation and oppression. Crime, with its many historical variations, is an integral part of class struggle in the development of capitalism.

Following Marx and Engels' limited and brief discussion, criminals outside the capitalist class are usually viewed as being among the lumpenproletariat.[31] Accordingly, criminals of the oppressed classes are regarded as unproductive workers; they are parasitical in that they do not

30. Steven Spitzer, "Toward a Marxian Theory of Deviance," *Social Problems* 22 (June 1975): 638–51.
31. Karl Marx and Frederick Engels, *The Communist Manifesto* (New York: International Publishers, 1965; original 1848), p. 20.

contribute to the production of goods, and they create a livelihood out of commodities produced by the working class.[32] Much criminal activity in the course of accommodation would thus appear to be an expression of false consciousness, an apolitical expression, an individualistic reaction to the forces of capitalist production.

Many crimes of accommodation are of this lumpen nature. Nevertheless, these actions occur within the context of capitalist oppression, stemming from the existing system of production. Much criminal behavior is of a parasitical nature, including burglary, robbery, drug dealing, and hustling of various sorts.[33] These are the *predatory crimes*. The behavior, although pursued out of the need to survive, is a reproduction of the capitalist system. The crimes are nevertheless antagonistic to the capitalist order. Most police activity is directed against these crimes.

In addition to the predatory crimes there are the *personal crimes* that are usually directed against members of the same class. These are the conventional criminal acts of murder, assault, and rape. They are pursued by those who are already brutalized by the conditions of capitalism. These actions occur in immediate situations that are themselves the result of more basic accommodations to capitalism.

Aside from these lumpen crimes, there are those actions carried out largely by the working class that are in resistance to the capitalist system. These actions, sometimes directed superficially against the work situation, are direct

32. Hirst, "Marx and Engels on Law, Crime and Morality," pp. 49–52; Ian Taylor, Paul Walton, and Jock Young, *The New Criminology: For a Social Theory of Deviance* (London: Routledge & Kegan Paul, 1973), pp. 217–20.
33. Judah Hill, *Class Analysis: United States in the 1970's* (Emeryville, Calif.: Class Analysis, 1975), pp. 86–87.

reflections of the alienation of labor—a struggle, however conscious or unconscious, against the exploitation of the life and activity of the worker. For example, workers may engage in concrete political actions against their employers:

> On the assembly lines of the American automobile industry, this revolt extends as far as clandestine acts of sabotage against a product (the automobile body) which appears to the worker as the detestable materialization of the social uselessness and individual absurdity of his toil. Along the same lines is the less extreme and more complex example of miners fighting with admirable perseverance against the closing of the mines where they are exploited under inferior human and economic conditions—but who, individually, have no difficulty in recognizing that even if the coal they produced were not so bad and so expensive, their job, under the pervailing conditions, would still be abominable.[34]

These defensive actions by workers are likely to become even more politically motivated and organized in the future. For built into the capitalist economy is the contradiction that increased economic growth necessitates the kind of labor that further alienates workers from their needs. Further economic expansion can only bring with it increased crimes of resistance. For the purpose of class struggle, leading to socialist revolution, a Marxist analysis of crime gives attention to the crimes of resistance, committed primarily by members of the working class.

The effects of the capitalist mode of production for the worker are all-inclusive, going far beyond the workplace itself. The worker can no longer be at home anyplace in the everyday world. The alienation experienced in the workplace now represents the condition of the worker in all other areas of life. Ownership and control of life in

34. Gorz, *Strategy for Labor*, pp. 57–58.

general have been surrendered to alien hands.[35] The production of life itself under capitalism is alienated. Furthermore, the natural productive process, of which work is central, has become restricted in the stages of capitalist accumulation. The increasing alienation of work, as Harry Braverman notes,

> consists in the narrowing of the base of productive labor upon which the economy rests, to the point where an ever smaller portion of society labors to maintain all of it, while the remainder is drafted, at lower rates of pay and even more demeaning conditions of labor, into the unproductive economy of capitalism. And finally, it consists in the misery of unemployment and of outright pauperization, which are aspects of the reserve army of labor created by capital more or less automatically in the accumulation process.[36]

Furthermore, a large portion of workers under advanced capitalism become expendable. For the capitalist the problem becomes that of the kind and size of labor force necessary to maximize production and realize surplus value. The physical well-being and spiritual needs of the worker are not the concern; rather, capitalism requires an "industrial reserve army" that can be called into action when necessary and relieved when no longer needed–but always available. Marx observed in *Capital:*

> But if a surplus laboring population is a necessary product of accumulation or of the development of wealth on a capitalist basis, this surplus population becomes, conversely, the lever of capitalist accumulation, nay, a condition of existence of the capitalist mode of production. It forms an industrial reserve army that belongs to capital quite as absolutely as

35. Karl Marx, *The Grundrisse,* ed. David McLellan (New York: Harper & Row, 1971), pp. 132–43.
36. Harry Braverman, "Work and Unemployment," *Monthly Review* 27 (June 1975): 30.

> if the latter had bred it at its own cost. Independently of the limits of the actual increase of population, it creates for the changing needs of the self-expansion of capital a mass of human material always ready for exploitation.[37]

Under these conditions, "the labor force consists of two parts, the employed and the unemployed, with a gray area in between, containing the part-time or sporadically employed. Furthermore, all these categories of workers and potential workers continuously expand or contract with technological change, the ups and downs of the business cycle, and the vagaries of the market, all inherent characteristics of capitalist production."[38] Many workers are further exploited by being relegated to the degradations and uncertainities of a reserve army of labor.

For the unemployed, as well as for those who are always uncertain about their employment, the life condition has its personal and social consequences. Basic human needs are thwarted when the life-giving activity of work is lost or curtailed. This form of alienation gives rise to a multiplicity of psycho-social maladjustments and psychic disorders.[39] In addition, unemployment means the loss of personal and family income. Choices, opportunities, and even life maintenance are jeopardized. For many people, the appropriate reaction consists not only of mental disturbance but also of outright acts of personal and social destruction.

Although the statistical evidence can never show conclusively the relation between unemployment and crime, largely because such statistics are politically constructed in

37. Karl Marx, *Capital* (Chicago: C. H. Kerr, 1932), p. 693.
38. Editors, "The Economic Crisis in Historical Perspective," *Monthly Review* 26 (June 1975): 2.
39. K. William Kapp, "Socio-Economic Effects of Law and High Employment," *Annals of the American Academy of Political and Social Science* 418 (March 1975): 60–71.

the beginning to obscure the failings of a capitalist economy, there is sufficient observation to recognize the obvious fact that unemployment produces criminality. Crimes of economic gain increase whenever the jobless seek ways to maintain themselves and their families. Crimes of violence rise when the problems of life are further exacerbated by the loss of life-supporting activity. Anger and frustration at a world that punishes rather than supports produce their own forms of destruction. Permanent unemployment–and the acceptance of that condition–can result in a form of life where criminality is an appropriate and consistent response.

Hence, crime under capitalism has become a response to the material conditions of life.[40] Nearly all crimes among the working class in capitalist society are actually a means of *survival,* an attempt to exist in a society where survival is not assured by other, collective means. Crime is inevitable under capitalist conditions.

Yet, understanding crime as a reaction to capitalist conditions, whether as acts of frustration or means of survival, is only one side of the picture. The other side involves the problematics of the *consciousness* of criminality in capitalist society.[41] The history of the working class is in large part one of rebellion against the conditions of capitalist production, as well as against the conditions of life resulting from work under capitalism. Class struggle involves, after all, a continuous war between two dialectically opposed interests: capital accumulation for the benefit of a nonworking minority class that owns and controls the means of production and, on the other hand, control and ownership of production by those who actually labor. Since

40. David M. Gordon, "Capitalism, Class, and Crime in America," *Crime and Delinquency* 19 (April 1973): 163–86.
41. Taylor, Walton, and Young, *New Criminology,* pp. 220–21.

the capitalist state regulates this struggle, the institutions and laws of the social order are intended to assure the victory of the capitalist class over the working class. Yet the working class constantly struggles against the capitalist class, as shown in the long history of labor battles against the conditions of capitalist production.[42] The resistance continues as long as there is need for class struggle, that is, as long as capitalism exists.

With the instruments of force and coercion on the side of the capitalist class, much of the activity in the working-class struggle is defined as criminal. Indeed, according to the legal codes, whether in simply acting to relieve the injustices of capitalism or in taking action against the existence of class oppression, actions against the interests of the state are crimes. With an emerging consciousness that the state represses those who attempt to tip the scales in favor of the working class, working-class people engage in actions against the state and the capitalist class. This is crime that is politically conscious.

Crimes of accommodation and resistance thus range from unconscious reactions to exploitation, to conscious acts of survival within the capitalist system, to politically conscious acts of rebellion. These criminal actions, moreover, not only cover the range of meaning but actually evolve or progress from *unconscious reaction* to *political rebellion*. Finally, the crimes may eventually reach the ultimate stage of conscious political action—*revolt*. In revolt, criminal actions are not only against the system but are also an attempt to overthrow it.

42. Sidney Lens, *The Labor Wars: From the Molly Maguires to the Sitdowns* (New York: Doubleday, 1973); Jeremy Brecher, *Strike!* (Greenwich, Conn.: Fawcett, 1972); Samuel Yellin, *American Labor Struggles* (New York: S. A. Russell, 1936); Richard O. Boyer and Herbert M. Morais, *Labor's Untold Story* (New York: Cameron Associates, 1955).

The movement toward a socialist society can occur only with political consciousness on the part of those oppressed by capitalist society. The alternative to capitalism cannot be willed into being but requires the conscious activity of those who seek new conditions of existence. Political consciousness develops in the realization of the alienation suffered under capitalism. The contradiction of capitalism—the disparity between actuality and human possibility—makes large portions of the population ready to act in ways that will bring about a new existence. When people become conscious of the extent to which they are dehumanized under the capitalist mode of production, when people realize the source and nature of their alienation, they become active in a movement to build a new society. Many of the actions taken result in behaviors that are defined as criminal by the capitalist state.

THE MEANING OF CRIME

A Marxist understanding of crime, as developed here, begins with an analysis of the political economy of capitalism. The class struggle endemic to capitalism is characterized by a dialectic between domination and accommodation. Those who own and control the means of production, the capitalist class, attempt to secure the existing order through various forms of domination, especially crime control by the capitalist state. Those who do not own and control the means of production, especially the working class, accommodate and resist in various ways to capitalist domination.

Crime is related to this process. Crime control and criminality (consisting of the crimes of domination and the crimes of accommodation) are understood in terms of the conditions resulting from the capitalist appropriation of labor. Variations in the nature and amount of crime occur in the course of developing capitalism. Each stage in the development of capitalism is characterized by a particular pattern of crime. The meaning and changing meanings of crime are found in the development of capitalism.

What can be expected in the further development of capitalism? The contradictions and related crises of capitalist political economy are now a permanent feature of advanced capitalism. Further economic development along capitalist lines will solve none of the internal contradictions of the capitalist mode of production.[43] The capitalist state must, therefore, increasingly utilize its resources—its various control and repressive mechanisms—to maintain the capitalist order. The dialectic between oppression by the capitalist class and the daily struggle of survival by the oppressed will continue—and at an increasing pace.

The only lasting solution to the crisis of capitalism is, of course, socialism. Under late, advanced capitalism, socialism will be achieved only in the struggle of all people who are oppressed by the capitalist mode of production, namely, the workers and all elements of the surplus population. An alliance of the oppressed must take place.[44] Given the objective conditions of a crisis in advanced capitalism, and the conditions for an alliance of the oppressed, a mass socialist movement can be formed, cutting across all divisions within the working class.

The objective of Marxist analysis is to lead to further questioning of the capitalist system, leading to an improved understanding of the consequences of capitalist development. The *ultimate meaning* of crime in the development of capitalism is the need for a socialist society. And as the

43. Ernest Mandel, "The Industrial Cycle in Late Capitalism," *New Left Review* 90 (March–April 1975): 3–25.
44. O'Connor, *Fiscal Crisis of the State,* pp. 221–56.

preceding discussion indicates, in moving toward the socialist alternative, our study of crime is necessarily based on an economic analysis of capitalist society. Crime is essentially a product of the contradictions of capitalism. Crime is sometimes a force in social development: when it becomes a part of the class struggle, increasing political consciousness. But our real attention must continue to be on the capitalist system itself. Our understanding is furthered as we investigate the nature, sources, and consequences of the development of capitalism. As we engage in this work, the development of socialism becomes more evident.

3
CLASS STRUGGLE AND THE CAPITALIST STATE

The growth of capitalism increasingly divides society into opposing classes—those who own and control the means of production and those who do not, those who appropriate labor power and those who sell their labor power. A political economy based on surplus value is characterized by an inevitable class struggle between a capitalist class and a working cláss. And in the further accumulation of capital, the capitalist class requires the expanded productivity of workers and the further appropriation of surplus value. The dynamic of capitalism is the struggle between classes.

A class analysis, based on the underlying political economy, is a necessary beginning in a Marxist understanding of crime. Nevertheless, new questions are emerging that must be answered before an adequate analysis is possible.

These questions are prompted largely by the transformation of capitalism into its late stage of development. Thus, in addition to the general question of the nature of advanced capitalism, there are questions that involve (1) the changing class structure of advanced capitalism; (2) the increasing development and importance of the capitalist state; (3) the class character of the state and how it operates as a capitalist state; (4) the control apparatus of the capitalist state, especially the processes of crime and control; and (5) the problematics of legitimation and consciousness in late capitalism, relating particularly to the changing nature of criminality. In considering these questions we seek answers that allow us both to understand crime today and to contribute to a politics of socialist struggle and revolution.

CLASS STRUCTURE OF ADVANCED CAPITALISM

Class analysis of contemporary society takes us beyond the radical social theories of the recent past. While "elite theory" allowed us to move beyond pluralist notions of society and politics, it stopped short of a Marxist methodology and conception of the dynamics of change and revolution. A theory that posits an opposition between an elite (or a "ruling class") and the "masses" (or "the people") fails to provide an adequate understanding of the forces of capitalist society. In elite theory, the primary element is the interest of the elite in maintaining the status quo. Class analysis, in comparison, begins with the fundamental dynamic of capitalism: the dialectic between two opposing forces–preservation of the existing relationships and modification or destruction of these relationships. *Class* is thus the necessary concept in a Marxist analysis of the inner working of capitalist society.

> That is to say, for Marx the concept of "class" was inseparably linked to a dialectical theory of social change; "class" was not primarily a category for describing how a particular capitalist society looked at any given point in time, but rather above all an analytic tool for elucidating the sources of structural change within the capitalist system, a theory of the direction in which capitalist societies were developing. This is why the Marxist model of capitalist society is normally a two-class model: the two classes represent the two sides of a fundamental contradiction which is assumed to be the source of conflicts sufficiently important to produce significant structural change. In short, the assumption of two classes–a superordinate class and a subordinate class–defined in dialectical opposition to each other is the starting point for Marx's theory of social change and revolution.[1]

We begin class analysis with the recognition that (1) classes are an expression of the underlying forces of the capitalist mode of production and that (2) classes are not fixed entities but rather ongoing processes. Analytically it is important to describe the class structure of capitalist society, but in reality classes are the internal forces of capitalism, in ever-changing transitional and dialectical relation. This is to be remembered especially when we attempt to place persons and occupational groups into class categories. For purposes of political struggle we inevitably think and act concretely. We must realize, however, that defining the place of particular elements in the process of capitalism "cannot always be solved neatly and definitively,

1. Isaac Balbus, "Ruling Elite Theory vs. Marxist Class Analysis," *Monthly Review* 23 (May 1971): 37–38.

nor, it should be added, does science require that it must be so solved."[2] What is important to understand are the motive forces of capitalism that make classes and class relations necessary.

Since capitalism is constantly transforming itself, it follows that class analysis must be attuned to the changes in class relations that occur in the development of capitalism. Although all stages of capitalist development involve a dialectic between ownership and nonownership, control and noncontrol, domination and resistance, the fundamental opposition between the capitalist class and the working class continues. Yet it is becoming apparent that a class analysis of advanced capitalism requires a more elaborate description of this relationship. The class structure of advanced capitalism is in transition; new forms are emerging within the dynamic of the capitalist mode of production. Needed now is a class analysis, which we can use in our study of crime, that characterizes the advanced stage of capitalism.

The principal classes of any capitalist society, at the various stages of development, are the classes whose interrelations determine the essence of the mode of production.[3] In addition, there are the fractions (or secondary classes) *within* the primary classes that either have survived from previous modes and levels of production or are emerging in the existing system. The composition of the principal classes has been undergoing changes in recent decades of capitalist development. These changes are connected with

2. Harry Braverman, *Labor and Monopoly Capital: The Degradation of Work in the Twentieth Century* (New York: Monthly Review Press, 1974), p. 409.
3. L. Afanasyev et al., *The Political Economy of Capitalism* (Moscow: Progress Publishers, 1974), p. 22.

modern scientific and technological advances and with the new demands of capitalist accumulation.

The developments in capitalism are of such major proportion that some theorists suggest that the classical Marxist formulations need to be rejected or at least modified considerably.[4] Much debate revolves around the extent to which the labor theory of value applies in advanced capitalist society. It is being argued that science and technology are today the leading productive forces and the major sources of value.[5]

But more important in the development of advanced capitalism is the expansion of the working class. A proletariatization of the labor force is occurring, brought about by shifts in the nature of work (from manual to clerical, service, and commercial work) and by increasing portions of the labor force being employed in the state sector. Changes in the class structure of advanced capitalism force us to think again about class and to employ a class analysis in our understanding of concrete problems.

The starting point in a description of class structure is the recognition, made by Marx, that class structure on the *abstract* level is a consequence of the level of development of the capitalist mode of production.[6] On the abstract level, class structure is an expression of the struggle of classes, the antagonistic relation between those who own and con-

4. For example, see Jurgen Habermas, *Theory and Practice,* trans. John Viertel (Boston: Beacon Press, 1974), pp. 253–82; and James Farganis, "A Preface to Critical Theory," *Theory and Society* 2 (Winter 1975): 483–508.
5. This argument is critiqued in Peter Laska, "A Note on Habermas and the Labor Theory of Value," *New German Critique* 1 (Fall 1974): 154–62.
6. Theotonio Dos Santos, "The Concept of Social Class," *Science and Society* 34 (Summer 1970): 166–93.

trol the means of production and those who do not. This is the dialectic of classes, in the context of the contradictions of the internal workings of the capitalist mode of production.

Empirically, however, in the *concrete* analysis of specific societies at a particular point in history, the class structure is much more complex. Theotonio Dos Santos has written: "A concrete, historically given society cannot correspond directly to abstract categories. As we have said, Marxism does not use abstraction formally. After it has elaborated the concept abstractly, it later denies it, showing the limitation of this level of the concept. Hence, the need for passing to more concrete levels of abstraction."[7] In the analysis of a given society at a specific time, then, a description of class structure may be quite elaborate. The primary focus, nevertheless, is on the nature of the class structure in relation to the level of capitalist development.

In constructing a concrete class structure, utilizing the labor theory of value, the population is divided according to its production of commodities for capitalism. *Productive* labor under capitalism, as defined by Marx in his *Theories of Surplus-Value* and the fourth volume of *Capital,* consists of labor that produces commodity value for capital.[8] That is, money is exchanged for labor with the purpose of appropriating that value which it creates over and above what is paid, the *surplus* value. *Unproductive* labor, in comparison, is labor that is not exchanged for capital and that does not produce any surplus value, hence, profit, for capitalists.[9] Clerical, sales, and service workers (primarily em-

7. Ibid., p. 177.
8. The Marxist formulation of productive and unproductive labor is discussed at length in Ian Gough, "Marx's Theory of Productive and Unproductive Labour," *New Left Review* 76 (November–December 1972): 47–72.
9. See Braverman, *Labor and Monopoly Capital,* pp. 410–15.

ployed in the government and in corporations) make up the greatest portion of unproductive labor. Moreover, there are those persons, primarily the self-employed, who fall outside of the distinction between productive and unproductive labor because they are outside the capitalist mode of production. Unproductive labor, that used by the capitalist for "unproductive" purposes, is increasing significantly under advanced capitalism.

The needs of capital for unproductive labor have grown remarkably. "The more productive capitalist industry has become—that is to say, the greater the mass of surplus value it extracts from the productive population—the greater has become the mass of capital seeking its shares in this surplus. And the greater the mass of capital, the greater the mass of unproductive activities which serve only the diversion of this surplus and its distribution among various capitals."[10] But most important, the mass of workers now included in unproductive labor has been transformed into a modern commercial proletariat. This wage-working segment has become a major element in the capitalist mode of production. In the process, they have lost many of the characteristics that formerly separated them from the traditional productive workers. As Braverman has shown, their growth in the labor force has brought them into the modern proletariat:

> When they were few they were unlike productive labor, and having become many they are like productive labor. Although productive and unproductive labor are technically distinct, although productive labor has tended to decrease in proportion as its productivity has grown, while nonproductive labor has increased *only as a result* of the increase in surpluses thrown off by productive labor—despite these

10. Ibid., p. 415.

> distinctions, the two masses of labor are not otherwise in striking contrast and need not be counterposed to each other. They form a continuous mass of employment which, at present and unlike the situation in Marx's day, has everything in common.[11]

Advanced capitalism is also creating another segment within the class structure. As the struggle over the rate of surplus value continues, and is increased by economic crises that cause rates of profit to fall, there is the construction of an "industrial reserve army." [12] The major portion of the unemployed labor force stands in reserve for employment when capitalists need their labor power. Among this reserve are the unemployed, the officially counted part of the relative surplus working population that is necessary for advanced capitalism. The estimation of unemployment at any given time is as high as 13 million.[13] And this figure does not include the large number of workers who do not receive enough pay to support a family above the subsistence level and must therefore attempt to find additional work.

Thus, the relative surplus population, in the reserve army, takes a variety of forms under advanced capitalist production. The reserve army includes: "the unemployed; the sporadically employed; the part-time employed; the mass of women who, as houseworkers, form a reserve for the 'female occupations'; the armies of migrant labor, both agricultural and industrial; the black population with its extraordinarily high rates of unemployment; and the foreign reserves of labor." [14] Added to this combined reserve

11. Ibid., p. 423.
12. Ernest Mandel, "The Industrial Cycle in Late Capitalism," *New Left Review* 90 (March–April 1975): 3–25.
13. Editors, "Capitalism and Unemployment," *Monthly Review* 27 (June 1975): 11.
14. Braverman, *Labor and Monopoly Capital,* p. 386.

army are those millions of workers who no longer have a chance of ever being fully or even partly employed. No longer able to search for jobs, they are forced on to the welfare rolls. The size of the pauperized mass is now about 15 million persons.[15] This is the segment of the working class that readily turns to crime in the struggle for survival.

What, then, to continue our discussion of class structure, does the class structure of advanced capitalist society look like? The argument I am making is that the development of capitalist economy requires changes in the forces and relations of production. But this *does not* mean that there is a basic change in the basic economic relations between classes. While the class composition changes, around new forms of economic activity and occupations, capitalist development does not give rise to new classes within capitalism. Rather, it gives rise to what Marx described as *fractions* within classes.[16] The basic dialectic between the capitalist class and the working class still predominates, but added to this is a dialectic between divisions within these classes.

The expansion of capital necessitates divisions within the classes. These new fractions are of such importance that several class theorists have posited the formation of a new class of "petty bourgeoisie" (including civil servants, intellectuals, and other unproductive workers).[17] While

15. Harry Braverman, "Work and Unemployment," *Monthly Review* 27 (June 1975): 30.
16. I am following the argument presented by Francesca Freedman, "The Internal Structure of the American Proletariat: A Marxist Analysis," *Socialist Revolution* 5 (October–December 1975): 41–83.
17. Nicos Poulantzas, *Classes in Contemporary Capitalism* (London: New Left Books, 1975); and Anthony Giddens, *The Class Structure of the Advanced Societies* (New York: Harper & Row, 1975). Also see Nicos Poulantzas, "On Social Classes," *New Left Review*, no. 78 (March–April 1973): 27–54.

the subjective consciousness of the petty bourgeoisie may be different from that of the industrial working class, this does not mean that the fundamental objective antagonism of the capitalist mode of production has been altered in any important way. As Francesca Freedman has written, "The subjective and objective must be united in a dialectical manner for a dynamic analysis of classes, since classes are in their essence the expression of the antagonistic contradictions upon which a mode of production is based. Thus, class struggle is the highest form in which these contradictions are expressed." [18] The class struggle between the working class and the capitalist class continues, and continues at even a faster and higher level, under advanced capitalism.

The fractioning of the working class is taking place in response to the development of different sectors of the economy.[19] This century has seen a tremendous shift in relative and absolute numbers from industrial to nonindustrial labor. The service producers (including professional and technical, clerical and sales, and service workers) have experienced a steady growth while manual workers have declined. Shifts in the economic sectors are reflections of the advancing forms of capitalist production and accumulation.

Moreover, fractions within the working class are occurring along hierarchical lines, ranging from the industrial reserve army at the bottom to the various levels of the labor force.[20] Included in the labor force hierarchy are (1) the

18. Freedman, "Internal Structure of the American Proletariat," p. 47.
19. Ibid., pp. 54–56.
20. Ibid., pp. 56–67. On the overwhelming proportion of minorities and women in the unskilled, service, and office occupations, see Martin Oppenheimer, "The Sub-Proletariat: Dark Skins and Dirty Work," *Insurgent Sociologist* 4 (Winter 1974): 7–20; and Al Szy-

unskilled workers in industrial, service, and office occupations—composed largely of minorities and women; (2) the skilled workers, industrial and nonindustrial; (3) the low- and middle-level technical workers, including teachers and nurses; and (4) the middle-level management personnel, salaried professionals, university professors, and middle-level government bureaucrats. The hierarchical fracturing of the working class enforces class discipline and division, thus reproducing class relations under capitalism.

Contrary to the conventions of social science, managerial personnel are dialectically a part of the working class, albeit at the top of the hierarchy. While corporate managers, in particular, occupy a tenuous position, not owning the means of production but sometimes controlling other aspects of the labor force, they are workers in comparison to the capitalists.

Managers, as Marx observed, are the agents of the capitalist class: "An industrial army of workmen under the command of a capitalist requires, like a real army, officers (managers) and sergeants (foremen, overseers) who, while work is being done, command in the name of the capitalist." [21] These "supervisory" workers are themselves subject to a definite market price. Therefore, Freedman notes:

> It must be re-emphasized here that *middle-level management* is part of the working class. Although these managers may be highly paid, their income is insufficient to allow them entry into the capitalist class—i.e., they cannot own signifi-

---

manski, "The Socialization of Women's Oppression: A Marxist Theory of the Changing Position of Women in Advanced Capitalist Society," *Insurgent Sociologist* 6 (Winter 1976): 31–58.

21. Quoted in Freedman, "Internal Structure of the American Proletariat," p. 65. From Karl Marx, *Capital* (New York: International Publishers, 1967), 1:322.

> cant amounts of corporate stock or other financial assets. Moreover, their income depends upon work, upon their receiving a salary. In contrast, the top ranks of management are drawn from the capitalist class itself; the fact that top-level managers receive a salary is not enough to put them into the ranks of the working class, since in this case the wage is merely a "juridical" relation.[22]

This is where the working class ends in the class structure and the capitalist class begins.

The capitalist class is actually composed of relatively few people. In terms of the ownership of wealth, for example, 1.6 percent of the population owns 80 percent of all corporate stocks and government bonds.[23] According to occupation, only slightly over 1 percent of the labor force is composed of corporate owners and top-level managers. Some studies have shown that the capitalist class (or the "bourgeoisie," or the "ruling class") composes about 1.5 percent of the population, including the wives and children of the men who own and control the major units of the economy.[24] Furthermore, members of this class dominate the boards, commissions, and committees that control the economic, social, and political institutions of the country.[25] The lack of information about the capitalist class is not due to happenstance, as Judah Hill observes:

> It is very difficult to get accurate information about this class. They use all the resources at their command to keep

22. Ibid., pp. 65–66.
23. Robert J. Lampman, *The Share of Top Wealth-Holders in National Wealth, 1922–1956* (Princeton, N.J.: Princeton University Press, 1956).
24. Judah Hill, *Class Analysis: United States in the 1970's* (Emeryville, Calif.: Class Analysis, 1975), p. 4.
25. See G. William Domhoff, *The Higher Circles: The Governing Class in America* (New York: Random House, 1970).

> secret the extent of their power, their decisions, who they are, etc. There are two main reasons for this. One is that they don't like to pay taxes; thus it is in their interest to keep hidden the extent of their wealth and income. More important is their desire to perpetuate the myth that America is a free, classless society. As long as the existence of a ruling class is hidden, the chances of rebellion against it are small. The myth that America is a "pluralistic Democracy" is one of the greatest weapons in the arsenal that maintains their class rule.[26]

The capitalist class also is divided into several fractions. Two major fractions are those capitalists who own and control the major units of the economy in comparison to those whose holdings and power are less than that of the uppermost sector of the capitalist class. The upper division, the "monopoly sector," as contrasted to the "lieutenant sector," owns the largest corporations and financial institutions, the names of the DuPonts, Rockefellers, Mellons, and Fords being characteristic of this sector.[27] Today the capitalists of the upper division control or influence world economy. The other segment, comprising about 1 percent of the total 1.5 percent population of the capitalist class, is largely delegated power by the monopoly sector. Their ownership and control are less permanent and not as pervasive. Their economic control is on the regional and state level, in contrast to the national and international realm. However, this sector of the capitalist class wields political power as U.S. senators, governors, cabinet officials, directors of the CIA, and President.

Other fractions, other than these two, develop in the capitalist class as new contradictions and needs arise in

26. Hill, *Class Analysis,* pp. 4–5.
27. Ibid., pp. 5–9.

advanced capitalism. Moreover, there are further divisions within the capitalist class, along such lines as how to maintain capitalist rule. *Structurally,* however, the capitalist class acts as a whole in securing and perpetuating capitalism. The purpose of the capitalist class is to make the world safe for the capitalist mode of production.

Finally, in table 1, based on the above discussion, is the class structure of advanced capitalism as represented in the United States. The striking fact is that the overwhelming proportion of the population of advanced capitalism consists of the working class.[28] In spite of talk about the "new middle class" and the "new working class," the objective condition is the further reproduction of the working class. Although an increasing portion of the labor force is employed in the service and office sectors of the economy, it is doing unskilled work. And an ever increasing proportion of the population is being relegated to the reserve army and the pauperized poor. Advanced capitalism produces a surplus population, a population that is denied work. As this occurs, criminality increasingly becomes an alternative for an enlarging segment of the population.

At the same time, with the growth of the service, sales, and office sectors, a large portion of the working class is coming to share the same general conditions of the industrial proletariat. The nonindustrial fraction of the working class is going through a process of "proletarianization," coming more and more to approximate the conditions of the industrial proletariat. As this occurs, it is likely that "such sectors will, along with the industrial proletariat, form the pivotal elements of a revolutionary socialist movement." [29]

28. The proportions in the adult population are based on a composite of population and labor statistics, as gathered especially in Hill, *Class Analysis.*
29. Freedman, "Internal Structure of the Proletariat," p. 81.

TABLE 1. CLASS STRUCTURE OF THE UNITED STATES
(with estimated percentages of the adult population)

Class	Composition	
Capitalist Class 1.5%	Owns and controls production; wields state power	
Petty Bourgeoisie 18.5%	Professionals, middle management, bureaucrats	
	Technical—10% teachers, nurses, medical technicians	Technical and Skilled Working Class 25%
	Skilled—15% craftsmen, clerical, sales, operatives, transport, industrial	
Working Class 80%	Unskilled—30% industrial labor, service, office, sales, clerical	Unskilled Working Class 55%
	Reserve army—15% unemployed	
	Pauperized poor—10%	

Within the class structure of advanced capitalism is the dialectic that increases class struggle and the movement for socialist revolution.

THE CAPITALIST STATE

A theory of crime necessarily presupposes a theory of the state. Since it is through state policy that behavior is officially defined as criminal, any explanation of crime (including both crime control and criminality) also implies a theory of the nature of the state. In the official sense, the state controls social activity; and in the course of doing so, it defines as criminal that activity which violates the interests the state is promoting and protecting.

The question arises, then, as to the proper conception of the state for a Marxist understanding of criminal justice. The problem is especially crucial for us given the fact that a Marxist theory of the state is very much in a process of reformulation. As a beginning, following the traditional Marxian interpretation, the state is intimately tied to civil society, especially to the class structure. The state appears to rest on the material, economic base of society: thus the Marxian characterization of the capitalist state as the managing committee of the capitalist ruling class. But the state is more than a mere instrument of the capitalist class; it is a social reality itself.[30]

As Anthony Giddens has recently pointed out, Marx's writings on the nature of the relationship between society and the state contain a definite ambiguity:

> On the one hand, the theorem is advanced that the state is nothing more than the vehicle whereby the interests of the dominant class are realized: the state is merely an agency of class domination. On the other hand, many of Marx's comments upon the capitalist state show an awareness of the

30. See Amy Beth Bridges, "Nicos Poulantzas and the Marxist Theory of the State," *Politics and Society* 4 (Winter 1974): 161–90.

administrative significance of the state as the "supervisor" of the operations of capitalist production.[31]

Generally, however, Marx was showing that the state provides a framework for the class structure inherent in the capitalist mode of production. Yet there is a difference between a theory of the state as an *instrument* of class domination and the state as a *coordinating agency* responsible for the overall administrative operations of capitalist society. The theories that are currently being formulated are addressed to these problems and are themselves reflections of the changing nature of the state under advanced capitalism.

The recent Marxian formulations of the state go beyond the instrumentalist notion that sees the state and its policies as direct outcomes of manipulations by the ruling class. Also expanded is the structuralist theory that describes the functions the state performs to reproduce capitalist society as a whole. In like manner, the Hegelian-Marxist perspective that emphasizes consciousness and ideology is being made more concrete, materialist, and historical.[32] The complex apparatus of the state in late capitalism is becoming evident.

The advancing capitalist state is losing much of its superstructural character. "The state is increasingly involved in accumulation, not just to protect the conditions of accumulation as earlier Marxist thinking emphasized, but to participate actively in the creation of those conditions." [33] Thus,

31. Giddens, *Class Structure of the Advanced Societies,* p. 51.
32. On these traditions, see David A. Gold, Clarence Y. H. Lo, and Erik Olin Wright, "Recent Developments in Marxist Theories of the Capitalist State," *Monthly Review* 27 (October 1975): 29–43.
33. David A. Gold, Clarence Y. H. Lo, and Erik Olin Wright, "Recent Developments in Marxist Theories of the Capitalist State, Part 2," *Monthly Review* 27 (November 1975): 42.

the state itself is becoming a material force, a part of the substructure, at least a "middle structure." But more important, the state is seen dialectically, as an apparatus developing in relation to the accumulation of capital under the late stages of advanced capitalism. The internal organization of the state is problematical as it is being transformed in the course of the emerging contradictions of advanced capitalism. Class struggle itself, resulting from these contradictions, is transforming the state. The capitalist state is in transition.

The theoretical problem at this time is that of *linking* the class structure of advanced capitalism to the capitalist state. The starting point, as noted by Claus Offe, is the class character of the state.[34] That is, how is the capitalist state really a *capitalist* state and not merely a state in capitalist society? As Offe then shows, in an investigation of the internal structure of the capitalist state, several "selective mechanisms" within the state apparatus either exclude anticapitalist interests from entering into state policy or assure the inclusion of capitalist interests in state policy. These structural features "put the State in a position to formulate and express class-interests more appropriately and circumspectly than can be done by representatives of the class–in the form of isolated units of capital." [35] The state thereby provides the necessary conditions for the continued accumulation of capital. Moreover, in periods of political crisis, as the selective mechanisms begin to break down, the state is forced to rely more and more on *repression* in order

34. Claus Offe, "Class Rule and the Political System: On the Selectiveness of Political Institutions," mimeo, 1973. (A translation of chap. 3 of *Strukturprobleme des kapitalistischen Staates* [Frankfurt: Suhrkamp, 1972]).
35. Ibid., p. 8.

to maintain its class character. In acting negatively the state attempts to exclude interests and forces that oppose or threaten the capitalist system. Class structure is thus translated into political power in the structure and operation of the capitalist state.

The capitalist state of advanced capitalist society, while still related to the underlying political economy, is developing a greater amount of autonomy. Rather than being a simple instrument for specific capitalists, it is becoming a complex apparatus with its own direction and its own contradictions. And as the capitalist state continues to develop, a "fiscal" crisis becomes endemic. The growth of the state and the ensuing crisis have been analyzed by James O'Connor in *The Fiscal Crisis of The State*.[36] A major part of his argument can be summarized as follows:

> There is the recognition that the capitalist state must attempt to perform two contradictory functions–accumulation and legitimation. The state attempts to support the accumulation of private capital while trying to maintain social peace and harmony. Since accumulation is crucial to the reproduction of the class structure, legitimation necessarily involves attempts to mystify the process and to repress or manage discontent. Both accumulation and legitimation are translated into demands for state activity. But while this implies an increase in state expenditures, the revenues for meeting these needs are not always forthcoming, since the fruits of accumulation (greater profits) are not socialized. This is the fiscal crisis.[37]

36. James O'Connor, *The Fiscal Crisis of the State* (New York: St. Martin's Press, 1973).
37. Gold, Lo, and Wright, "Recent Development in Marxist Theories of the Capitalist State, Part 2," p. 41. Also see San Francisco Bay Area Kapitalistate Group, "The Fiscal Crisis of the State: A Review," *Kapitalistate*, no. 3 (Spring 1975): 149–57.

The state is thus an integral element in the accumulation process. It is one sector, that sector which includes production organized by the state itself. The expenditures of the *state sector* usually do not directly produce surplus value, however, but aid private capitalists in their capital accumulation, mainly by creating (as through education) the conditions for private accumulation. The *monopoly sector*, on the other hand, as the prime accumulating sector of the economy, generates technical advances and the expansion of capital. The *competitive sector* grows with the development of the monopoly sector, employing those who would otherwise be relegated to a surplus population because of economic development. The three sectors are highly interdependent, with the state attempting to sustain profits and hold the country together, performing both an accumulation function and a legitimation function. Economically the state cannot satisfy these requirements of advanced capitalism—thus crisis is basic to the capitalist state. Whether the state can continue to reproduce capitalism—both through its own entry into economic production and through the creation of the conditions for capitalist accumulation—is problematic, that is, dialectical.

Maintaining *social peace* while promoting the capitalist social order is both a costly and problematic task. The capitalist state must increasingly rely on the repressive elements of the state apparatus. Through its legal institutions (especially the police, courts, and corrections) the state seeks defensively to secure its own existence. The overall structure of dominance in late capitalism is determined as much by the crisis of the advanced state as it is by the political economy. While authority under liberal capitalism is drawn sharply along class lines, authority under late capitalism becomes state-centered, easily obscuring the class basis of political domination. Offe writes, "The late capitalist welfare state bases its legitimacy on the postulate of a universal participation in consensus formation and on the unbiased opportunity for all classes to utilize the state's services and to benefit from its regulatory acts of intervention."[38] As capitalism develops, the advanced state becomes a force in itself, an apparatus in the class struggle.

The state in advanced capitalism, therefore, is not simply an instrument for promoting the interests of a ruling class. Instead, the state secures the whole order of capitalism. Offe and Volker Ronge observe:

> The state does not patronize certain interests, and is not allied with certain classes. Rather, what the state protects and sanctions is a set of *rules* and *social relationships* which are presupposed by the class rule of the capitalist class. The state does not defend the interests of one class, but the common interests of all members of a *capitalist class society*.[39]

Thus, relating to the dynamics of class struggle is a new technocratic (and authoritarian) concept of politics, "a concept whose intention is no longer the seeing through of correct and just vital reforms, but the conservation of social relations which claim mere functionality as their justification."[40] There is the rise of a technocratic rationality in the late stage of capitalist development. It is embodied in the capitalist state and in its policies and practices of social control.

Class struggle, then, is being elevated and transposed into political struggle. The capitalist state increasingly relies on political repression in the class struggle. For the working

38. Claus Offe, "Political Authority and Class Structures: An Analysis of Late Capitalist Societies," *International Journal of Sociology* 2 (Spring 1972): 81.
39. Claus Offe and Volker Ronge, "Theses on the Theory of the State," *New German Critique*, no. 6 (Fall 1975): 139.
40. Offe, "Political Authority and Class Structures," p. 103.

class, class struggle becomes a political struggle. Marx argued that the conditions of developing capitalism would force the proletariat to move its struggle outside of the factory and toward the state. Class struggle may continue to be the motive force of history, but that force is increasingly political and is more and more dominated by the dynamics of the capitalist state.

The advanced capitalist state is increasingly subject to contradictions and crises. Welfare state policies, rather than solving structural contradictions of capitalism, serve to exacerbate the problems and create new ones. The growing surplus population generated by the demands of advanced capitalism cannot be handled by the welfare state. What is being produced in advanced capitalist society is an enlarging reserve army of the unemployed and unemployable.[41] By its very nature, the welfare state generates more problems that it can solve. It cannot integrate the displaced population produced by the late capitalist mode of production. More state control and repression become necessary. The welfare state phase of the capitalist state is in transition.

What is emerging is a new strategy of capitalist state policy. The control function of the state is being revised and expanded. Embodied in this development, however, is a dialectic between increased control and resistance to that control. This occurs particularly in the realm where control is most explicitly practiced, in the service organizations of advanced capitalism and in the control of the surplus population of the working class.[42] The expanded function of the state is a source of crisis in itself. The attempt by the state to control the problems generated by late capitalism is the basis of increased social conflict and political struggle.

41. Claus Offe, "Advanced Capitalism and the Welfare State," *Politics and Society* 2 (Summer 1972): 479–88.

42. Offe and Ronge, "Theses on the Theory of the State," pp. 145–47.

Thus it is that crime control, characterized by the emergence of "criminal justice," increasingly becomes a prime locus of political struggle. The new policies of criminal justice signal the kinds of controls that have to be devised and instituted by the state in the late stage of capitalist development. And within these policies there is the dialectic of class struggle that inevitably dooms even this form of state control.

THE CRISIS OF LEGITIMATION

The growth of the capitalist state is both a source and product of the development of capitalism. In the late stage of capitalist development the state has expanded and increased its role in securing the capitalist system. The state is necessary at this stage to ensure capital accumulation. Moreover, the state must also cope with the surplus population that results from state monopoly capitalism. The modern capitalist state has achieved a character of its own in relation to the basic class struggle.

Yet the new capitalist state is bound by its own contradictions. Ultimately it cannot sustain private capital accumulation and, at the same time, legitimize the relations of advanced capitalism. On the economic level, the state cannot solve its own fiscal crisis that results from increasing state expenditures to assure private capital accumulation. On the level of legitimation, the state cannot continue to maintain its credibility as it fails to solve the problems that it either creates or expands in the promotion of the capitalist economy. Even its attempts at pacification through social services, on the one hand, and repression, on the other, are doomed to defeat both on the economic level and on the level of legitimation. The modern capitalist state, on several levels, is in crisis. It is a crisis that will continue to increase as long as the capitalist system ceases to be transformed into a socialist system.

As the state expands as the primary instrument for advancing capitalism, it will necessarily have to develop stronger and more pervasive means of dominating the population. If the problems inherent to late capitalism cannot be solved by state intervention (by assisting capital accumulation and providing social services), the population will have to be more effectively controlled. Thus it is that the crisis of late capitalism signals the development of a new mode of human domination.[43] This is a domination that is in the first instance ideological, in restricting our conception of life chances and the problems of capitalism. Furthermore, it is a domination that is exercised in the physical control of our daily lives, in the practice of criminal justice. The modern capitalist state is the agency of these forms of domination.

But, these facts notwithstanding, the dialectic of class struggle assures a conflict within capitalist society. The capitalist state, in not only failing to eliminate class struggle but in fact increasing it, contains the contradiction for its own ultimate demise. While expanding the function of the state means more state control, it also means that larger portions of the population become politicized. Especially for the "unproductive" segments of the population, the portion that does not reproduce itself through the productive labor market, there is increased involvement in the reproduction of the capitalist state—and the entire capitalist system. For state workers, students, the unemployed, welfare recipients, housewives, and criminals, a political con-

43. Trent Schroyer, *The Critique of Domination: The Origins and Development of Critical Theory* (New York: George Braziller, 1973), pp. 238–47.

sciousness develops around their condition, a consciousness that questions the legitimacy of the existing system.[44] The entire working class (productive and unproductive) is thus joined in a common political context.

A problem for the modern capitalist state is one of integrating the unproductive, nonsurplus value portion of the population into the system of capitalist domination. Excluded from the traditional relations of capitalist domination–in the market economy–this new and increasing segment nevertheless must be controlled.[45] The problem cuts two ways: first, lack of integration generates its own sources of political rebellion and, second, integration actually politicizes this segment in the way that the working class in general is politicized. Either way, the emergence of a new and increasing fraction of the working class produces yet another crisis in the capitalist system. This is a crisis of legitimation that promotes a critical consciousness and further mobilizes the working class. As the state attempts further to promote and regulate capitalism, it creates forms of work that cannot be successfully integrated into capitalist domination. The recourse for the state is domination through coercion, explicitly through crime control and criminal justice. For the worker, the capitalist system loses its legitimacy, and political actions becomes possible.

Thus, the capitalist state itself makes us political, making class struggle obviously a political struggle. Just as the capitalist economy appropriates our labor power, the capitalist state attempts to appropriate our political power. Politics within the capitalist state becomes alienated politics, just as work under capitalism becomes alienated work. The

44. Jurgen Habermas, *Legitimation Crisis* (Boston: Beacon Press, 1975), pp. 66–70.
45. Claus Offe, "The Abolition of Market Control and the Problem of Legitimacy," *Kapitalistate,* no. 1 (1973): 109–16.

nature of political alienation under capitalism has been described by Alan Wolfe in the following way:

> Politics in general represents the social relationships among people, the ways they co-operate and refuse to co-operate with each other. But in capitalist society politics is replaced by alienated politics, which can be defined as the process through which people in similar positions are separated from each other, forced to compete instead of to co-operate. At the same time, this alienated relationship returns to people as a higher authority, as something over which they are not expected to have any control. Hence–political institutions in capitalist society can be defined as those institutions responsible for absorbing the common power that people possess as members of a dominated but majoritarian social class and for using that power to rule them, that is, to exercise political power (their own political power) over them for purposes alienated from those people themselves.[46]

Moreover, continues Wolfe, the *capitalist state* is "the political institution which claims primary responsibility for reproducing alienated politics, that is, for maintaining a political system based upon the extraction and imposition of power from people." [47]

But this alienation produces the contradiction, in terms of the crisis of legitimacy: the capitalist state is weakened by its own domination. The capitalist state cannot continue to maintain its legitimacy–and successfully exercise domination–when its foundations are faulty. The natural desire for a complete, unalienated politics undermines the legitimacy of the capitalist state and creates a rebellion against

46. Alan Wolfe, "New Directions in the Marxist Theory of Politics," *Politics and Society* 4 (Winter 1974): 148.
47. Ibid.

the state. As workers attempt to regain their true political being, the capitalist state is rejected and the whole of our social, economic, and political life is transformed.

The problem in transformation, then, becomes one of developing a class consciousness in the political struggle. When and how, we may ask, does a consciousness develop among the working class? Given any objective condition, such as location in regard to state domination and the political economy of work, how does a consciousness emerge that leads to rebellion and revolution? How does a class, or a fraction of a class, become a *class for itself,* representing real class interests, rather than merely being a class in itself? [48] What makes for true consciousness, leading to correct political action?

The continuing task of a Marxist criminology is to answer such questions. The problems to which we must address ourselves are in respect to the meaning and significance of crime in the contemporary historical context of advanced capitalism. More specifically,

> To what extent is crime best understood as a form of individual, self-preservative adaptation to the oppressive and exploitative conditions of capitalism? And when does it mainly express or reflect these conditions? To what extent and in what instances does crime represent a revolt against these conditions, or some form of opposition to established authority? And similarly, when does increasing crime manifest or augment an intensification of the crisis of legitimacy? Finally, when—if ever—might crime somehow pre-figure a revolutionary transformation of society? [49]

48. Dos Santos, "Concept of Social Class" pp. 181–84.
49. John Ainlay, Review of Taylor, Walton, and Young's *The New Criminology* and *Critical Criminology, Telos,* no. 26 (Winter 1975–76): 225.

In considering these questions we place human activity in the context of political struggle.

CRIME AND CONSCIOUSNESS

A critical question necessarily being raised in an emerging Marxist analysis of crime involves the *consciousness* of those who are defined as criminal. Much of the behavior that is criminally defined by the capitalist legal system is carried out by those who are not engaged in the production of surplus value, by the surplus population. Questions about the political consciousness of the criminally defined are thus part of the larger issue of the development of political consciousness among an increasing fraction of the working class.

Combined with the problem of the consciousness of those who are defined as criminal is the question of the revolutionary potential of criminally defined activity. The early discussions in radical criminology tended to romanticize law-breaking, suggesting that most deviants were political by mere fact of violating the bourgeois rules of capitalist society.[50] The question must be approached dialectically, however, as indicated by Elliott Currie's review of the problem:

> For Marx, consciousness is *not* a given; consciousness is problematic, and a major task of Marxian theory has been to understand the conditions under which it emerges and the conditions under which it doesn't. It follows that a main task of Marxian theory of *deviance* is to uncover the conditions in which "deviance" becomes politically progressive and

50. Noted in Drew Humphries, "Report on the Conference of the European Group for the Study of Deviance and Social Control," *Crime and Social Justice* 1 (Spring–Summer 1974): 11–17.

> those in which it doesn't; the conditions in which deviance represents the beginnings of conscious political action, and those in which it is simply the action of people ground down by a system they neither understand nor challenge.[51]

The question thus becomes: Under what conditions is action, including criminality, a conscious political activity?

Analysis of the problematic nature of action and consciousness involves an investigation of several facets of the underlying political economy: (1) the historical conditions that produce exploitation and class oppression, (2) the bourgeois rules and legal order that emerge to maintain and regulate class domination and struggle, (3) the development of the conditions that promote the activities of those who are exploited and oppressed by the capitalist system, and (4) the rise of conscious revolutionary activity. It is in an understanding of the development of capitalist political economy that we begin to understand the interrelated questions regarding the problem of crime. Crime, with its many historical variations, is an integral part of the class struggle in the development of capitalism.

This is *not* to argue that the operations and contradictions of capitalism have consequence only for the working class, that capitalism produces criminality only in the working class and not in the capitalist class. The argument is that the development of capitalism increases the level of class struggle and produces in the working class the need for actions that may be defined as criminal by the capitalist class. In contrast, the crimes of the capitalist class, ranging from the denial of basic human rights to political assassination, are ways of perpetuating the capitalist system. These systematic actions are an integral part of capitalism and are

51. Elliott Currie, Review of Taylor, Walton, and Young's *The New Criminology*, *Crime and Social Justice* 2 (Fall–Winter 1974): 112.

important to its survival. Through a system of repressive relationships, the state and the capitalist class are able systematically to commit crimes against the working class. However, for the purpose of our analysis of the problematics of crime and consciousness, our attention is necessarily on the actions of members of the oppressed working class, those who do not own and control the means of production, and those who are excluded from the productive process.

As I have indicated throughout, the principal concepts for the analysis of the meaning of crime are those of class struggle, work, exploitation, and state power—all in relation to the underlying political economy. With the development of capitalism, and the necessary division of classes, the labor power of workers has been appropriated by the capitalist class. Workers, in losing control over the productive process, are forced to produce value over and above the value of their labor power, or are forced out of the productive process entirely. Furthermore, the total life situation of the working class is subject to capitalist control in an exploitation that is general and all-pervasive, affecting the life conditions of the worker. This exploitation increases with the development of capitalism.

We thus start with the idea that work is a central life activity, giving meaning to our overall as well as our daily existence. From this follows the notion that people are only relatively free at given times and in specific places, under particular material conditions, to work in ways that fulfill them personally and promote social existence. Consequently, when work is thwarted as a life-giving activity, the way is open for activity that is detrimental to self and others. At the same time, some of the behaviors that follow from alienated work are an attempt to set things right again. Some behavior is a conscious rebellion against exploitation and inhumane conditions. And there is the responsive activity which, in a reproduction of capitalism, is pursued for economic survival or gain. Activity of a criminal nature becomes a rational and likely possibility under the conditions of capitalism. All of this is to say that crime —including both crime control and criminality—is a *by-product* of the political economy of capitalism.

But is crime more than a by-product of capitalism? If more than a by-product, when and how does crime become a *force* in the class struggle? The question is crucial to a Marxist analysis of crime; the answer determines whether (or better, in what instances) criminality is to be considered as an active part in structuring social life and in the dynamics of social change. It is thus the consciousness of criminal behavior that becomes important in our investigation. For it is consciousness that gives behavior a rational purpose in human history.

For the working class there are several possibilities for breaking through the conditions of capitalism: "One possibility involves conscious, organized efforts aimed at the goal of eliminating capitalist society itself as the historical manifestation of the class contradiction. The other possibility involves crude, unconscious reactions against the social position of working class people in the form of evading bourgeois laws through criminal acts." [52] Actions thus range from unconscious reactions to exploitation, to conscious acts of survival, to politically conscious acts of rebellion.

The problem regarding criminality, therefore, becomes that of the consciousness of the working class. The problem is stated precisely as follows:

52. Falco Werkentin, Michael Hofferbert, and Michael Baurmann, "Criminology as Police Science or: 'How Old Is the New Criminology?'" *Crime and Social Justice* 2 (Fall–Winter 1974): 27.

> This means that the question must be pursued as to how to determine the concrete causes of behavior which in the social setting of the proletariat lead either to conscious class struggle on the one hand, or to conforming behavior or delinquent behavior on the other. In pursuing this question, it would be necessary to characterize the general conditions which under capitalist conditions contribute to the evolution of proletarian class consciousness and organized political praxis, and which contain as well, in their contradiction, the delusion of individuals and the hindering of the development of class struggle. Besides these general conditions, it would be necessary to characterize the specific circumstances which lead to the development of criminal behavior patterns within the proletariat. This implies that the intellectual interests of such an analysis must be measured against a critical understanding of science which is fundamentally oriented toward the principal necessity of the overthrow of capitalist ruling apparatus.[53]

In theoretically considering the problematics of consciousness of criminality we assist in the transformation of unconscious criminality into conscious political activity. The development of class consciousness and struggle is the goal of a Marxist analysis of crime.

Therefore, under what conditions in the development of capitalism is criminally defined behavior a conscious political activity? When is the behavior of the working class consciously bound up in the larger class struggle, whereby an attempt is consciously made to change the condition of exploitation and to remove the domination of the capitalist class? This is not to imply that consciousness is simply determined by material conditions of class experience. Rather, as E. P. Thompson argues, "Class-consciousness is the way in which these experiences are handled in

53. Ibid.

cultural terms: embodied in traditions, value-systems, ideas, and institutional forms. If the experience appears as determined, class-consciousness does not."[54] A political consciousness tends to develop under conditions of class oppression, but the specific form it takes and how it becomes manifested in either reactive or revolutionary activity varies in different times and places. During certain periods in specific places, especially in times of economic and institutional crisis under advanced capitalism, the oppressed realize their class affiliation, reject the capitalist's reified view of the world, and act to change their historical circumstances.[55] In a dialectical process, people change themselves, their consciousness, and their circumstances.

We already know about some aspects of the early phases of the development of political consciousness among the oppressed. In a series of studies, Eric Hobsbawm has investigated the action and consciousness of what he calls "primitive" or "archaic" forms of social agitation.[56] These forms are primitive in that they lack the organization and ideological characteristics of modern revolutionary movements and they occur among traditional groups of people that are in the process of adapting to a modern capitalist economy. The social forms of rebellion include banditry of the Robin Hood type, rural secret societies, various peasant revolutionary movements of the millennarian sort, preindustrial urban "mobs" and their riots, some labor religious sects, and early labor revolutionary organizations. In all cases,

54. E. P. Thompson, *The Making of the English Working Class* (New York: Random House, 1963), p. 10.
55. David Sallach, "Class Consciousness and the Everyday World in the Work of Marx and Schutz," *Insurgent Sociologist* 3 (Summer 1973): 35–36.
56. Eric Hobsbawm, *Primitive Rebels* (New York: W. W. Norton, 1959); Eric Hobsbawm, *Bandits* (New York, Dell, 1969).

even in the very early phases of political consciousness, even among "prepolitical" people, there is the potential of a revolutionary transformation of society.

Hobsbawm arranges the forms of social agitation in an order of increasing revolutionary ambition. Social banditry "is little more than endemic peasant protest against oppression and poverty: a cry for vengeance on the rich and the oppressors, a vague dream of some curb upon them, a righting of individual wrongs." [57] Moreover, social bandits "are peasant outlaws whom the lord and state regard as criminals, but who remain within peasant society, and are considered by their people as heroes, as champions, avengers, fighters for justice, perhaps even leaders of liberation, and in any case as men to be admired, helped and supported." [58] Especially in periods of tension and disruption, as in the transition from kinship society to agrarian capitalism, banditry may develop into a larger movement, becoming a force in changing the society.

However, it is in the urban or industrial social movements that we find a more clearly transitional phenomenon between primitive and modern rebellion. While the "mob" may be little more than the urban equivalent of social banditry, although capable of mobilizing a large portion of the population, the labor sects represent the next phase of revolutionary activity and consciousness.[59] Labor sects, although still not an organized industrial working class, are the forerunner of modern labor movements. In these early labor organizations, there are the beginnings of the modern movements that advance to modern socialism and communism. The labor movement, in a transition from primitive rebellion to modern rebellion, developed certain forms of

57. Hobsbawm, *Primitive Rebels,* p. 5.
58. Hobsbawm, *Bandits,* p. 13.
59. Hobsbawm, *Primitive Rebels,* pp. 126–49.

trade-union and cooperative organization, types of political organization such as mass parties, and specific programs and ideologies. The increasing potential for revolutionary transformation of society comes with the rise of political consciousness among the working and oppressed class in the development of modern capitalist society.

The specific role of criminality in the revolutionary process has been observed in recent historical investigations of eighteenth-century European movements. In a study of the laboring poor in France during the French Revolution, Jeffry Kaplow notes that while professional criminals of the time were merely reproducing the social arrangements of the old regime, those people who "occasionally and incidentally fell afoul of the law" provided a real threat to the establishment:

> To them crime was always a way of satisfying an immediate need when all other means had been exhausted, rather than the sole source of revenue or a way to get rich quickly. Their criminality was caused by the poverty and rootlessness endemic to urban centers in the old regime and may even be seen, in part, as a protest against that poverty. It was apolitical, but it may have been a stage through which the laboring poor had to pass on the way to political consciousness. When they attained it, they put away the childish and ultimately futile thing that is individual petty crime.[60]

Some criminality, in this historical context, may thus be a transition to the further development of political consciousness.

However, in the next century in France the urban poor who occasionally engaged in crime did not necessarily develop political consciousness or become revolutionaries. In

60. Jeffry Kaplow, *The Names of Kings: The Parisian Laboring Poor in the Eighteenth Century* (New York: Basic Books, 1972), p. 151.

a summary of several investigations of the subject, the urban poor and their criminality have been described as follows:

> They lived in a world of their own, by coping and by crime, and they lived by their own code, in their own way. Their ways cut them off from comfortable society, where politics made sense. Perhaps the preindustrial poor never developed much political consciousness. Perhaps they considered revolution a luxury that only the bourgeois could afford.[61]

Although a proletariat revolution is not going to be made by the bourgeoisie, it also appears that political consciousness does not easily develop out of the conditions of extreme oppression and that the criminality resulting from the brutalization is not usually political.

The revolutionary character of the working class, however, in relation to urban crime, was noted by Engels in his study of the conditions of the working class in mid-nineteenth-century England.[62] Engels saw in crime, at this stage in the capitalist development of England, all of its contradictory nature. Generally, criminality represents a response to the oppression of the working class. Engels describes much of this behavior as being committed by an underclass of the surplus population that includes people who have lost all hope of ever returning to work, vagabonds, beggers, paupers, and prostitutes. Yet from this mass of suffering Engels sees a kind of person emerging who, provoked by intense distress, revolts openly against society.

Throughout Engels' discussion there is the recognition that criminality is a primitive form of insurrection, a re-

61. Robert Darnton, "Poverty, Crime and Revolution," *New York Review of Books,* 2 October 1975, p. 22.
62. Frederick Engels, *The Condition of the Working Class in England in 1844,* trans. Florence Kelley Wischnewetzky (New York: J. W. Lovell, 1887).

sponse to deprivation and oppression. Criminality in itself is not a satisfactory form of politics. As Steven Marcus notes in his study of Engels' writing on crime:

> Crime is a primitive form of insurrection, driven by need and deprivations, an incomplete but not altogether mistaken response to a bad situation, and coming into active existence only by overcoming the resistance of inherited values and internalized sanctions. . . . Nevertheless, an inescapable part of the meaning of crime is its essential failure. It is insufficiently rational and excessively, or too purely, symbolic and symptomatic. Most of all, in it the criminal remains socially untransformed: he is still an isolated individual pursuing activities in an underground and alternate marketplace; if he is successful, he is a small-time entrepreneur; at best, he is the member or leader of a gang. In no instance is he capable of organizing a movement to withstand the institutional forces that are arrayed against him. He lives in a parallel and parasitic world whose horizon is bounded and obscured by the larger society upon which it depends.[63]

This is crime, as Engels recognized, in its early phase of development, before becoming a political force.

The initial failure of crime is contradicted by the fact that for some people criminality is the beginning of a conscious rebellion against capitalist conditions. In the larger context, as Engels realized, criminality is transitional, an action against brutalizing conditions, a possible stage in the development of political consciousness.[64] *If* criminally defined behavior becomes a conscious activity in the organization of workers, including the organization of those who are unemployed (in the surplus population), then crime

63. Steven Marcus, *Engels, Manchester, and the Working Class* (New York: Random House, 1974), pp. 223–24.
64. Ibid., pp. 224–26.

attains a political and revolutionary character. In conscious response to social and economic oppression, action that is defined by the state as criminal could become a part of the revolutionary process.

Pursuing these ideas, the next step in understanding the meaning of action in the development of capitalism consists of research on working-class life and exploitation in concrete situations in the development of modern capitalism. We may begin, following Thompson's lead, by investigating the ways in which an emerging working class adapts to the capitalist process of industrialization.[65] The ways that workers respond to increasing exploitation of their labor are related to the cultural traditions they bring to the workplace and the culture they subsequently create. At various points in the development of capitalism, and in concrete locations, we may investigate the struggles that workers engage in and the consciousness that they create. How, then, does this process relate to the crime control by the capitalist class and the criminality of the working class in these concrete settings?

The kind of research that must be done, with modifications and extensions, can be found in the historical studies of Herbert Gutman on the adaptation of workers to industrialization in American communities.[66] In general, in the industrialization of the United States, masses of low-paid workers were required and were supplied by the surplus populations immigrating from Europe and the farmers removed from American soil. Capitalists were then faced with the problem of extracting surplus labor from a population that was undisciplined for factory work. These new

65. Thompson, *Making of the English Working Class.*

66. Herbert G. Gutman, "Work, Culture, and Society in Industrializing America, 1815–1919," *American Historical Review* 78 (June 1973): 531–88.

workers brought with them traditions and ways of life that conflicted with the demands of factory labor. In a study of three time periods in American industrialization, Gutman shows that the cultural traditions that the diverse populations brought to each period shaped the adaptation and behavior of these workers. Gutman argues that this perspective "is especially important in examining the premodern work habits of diverse American men and women and the cultural sanction sustaining them in an alien society in which the factory and the machine grew more and more important." [67]

Workers in America resisted the exploitation of capitalist factory production. They drew on the resources of their preindustrial culture, particularly their religious heritage. Workers resisted, along with other townspeople, the tenet that ownership of production meant supremacy of a capitalist class. Moreover, as shown in research by Stephan Thernstrom, class consciousness and worker solidarity emerged when workers came to know each other in interaction and struggle over a period of time in a single factory or community.[68] Adaptation to capitalist exploitation *and* resistance, especially through criminality, can be investigated in studies of emerging working class life in the industrializing towns and cities of the United States.

The model for such study consists, *first,* of a description of the stage of capitalist development in which the study takes place, involving an overall understanding of the political economy of the period. For a study in the United States, we must understand the stages—and the specific

67. Ibid., p. 543.
68. Stephan Thernstrom, "Urbanization, Migration, and Social Mobility in Late Nineteenth-Century America," in *Towards a New Past,* ed. Barton J. Bernstein (New York: Random House, 1968), pp. 158–75.

stage—in the development of American capitalism. Once this is done, the *second* part of the investigation consists of locating the research in a particular community. Within this concrete research setting, historically and geographically located, we then focus on several interrelated topics: (1) the nature of production, including the technology in the factory; (2) the exploitation in the workplace; (3) the conditions of everyday life in the community; (4) the culture of the workers and their families; (5) the developing consciousness of the workers; (6) the control and repression of workers, both inside the factory and in the community, including legal control of crime; and finally (7) how the resistance of workers is manifested in criminality. Action is understood, then, in reference to the forms of working-class resistance—consciously pursued or otherwise—to the exploitation of labor power in the development of capitalism. Research must be conducted in concrete communities where capitalism is developing and a working class is emerging.

This is not the end of the investigation. We must carry our study into the present. This means that we have to be aware of the transformations that have taken place in the working class in the last several decades. Advanced capitalism has brought with it an actual increase in the size and proportion of the working class; and there has been a shift in the nature of the labor performed by workers. As Braverman has shown, the occupational structure is steadily changing, with a decreasing proportion of the working-class population employed in manufacturing and an increasing portion employed in service, clerical, and professional occupations.[69] Changes in the processes of capitalist production have brought about changes in the kinds of

69. Braverman, *Labor and Monopoly Capital*, pp. 377–402.

labor necessary for capitalist accumulation. Rather than the creation of a new "middle class," the redistribution of labor has meant the development of a new fraction within the working class, which has lost all former superiorities over industrial workers, in terms of its scales of pay, its employment in times of economic fluctuation, and its conditions of everyday life.

For the study of crime this means, first, that much of what is called "white-collar crime" is actually criminality that is committed in response to new forms of labor exploitation, and must be so explained. But more important, the range as well as the intensity of exploitation is actually increasing with the recent development of capitalism. An *increasing portion* of the population is subject to the exploitation of capitalist production. Research, therefore, must expand from the study of crime and exploitation in the industrial community to the study of crime in the office. Given the increasing range and intensity of exploitation required in the further development of capitalism, we cannot expect any reduction in the problem of crime. The development of capitalism only increases crime, increasing control by capitalists and resistance by workers.

THE RISE OF POLITICAL CONSCIOUSNESS

To the extent that crime is directed against members of the working class, crime remains counterrevolutionary. Much, if not most, crime continues to victimize those who are already oppressed by capitalism and does little more than reproduce the existing order. With the development of political consciousness, however, some criminally defined actions become a part of the revolutionary process. And in some cases crime itself, upon self-reflection and collective reflection, may lead to a political and revolutionary consciousness.

The problem becomes that of knowing what are the conditions that produce political actions and what are the criminally defined activities that are related to these actions. Moreover, as long as the capitalist class attempts to dominate, using its forms of legal repression, actions that threaten the established order will be defined by the capitalist state as criminal. In this sense, crime and political actions are inextricably linked.

Without the development of a political consciousness, criminality per se is an unstable factor in class struggle and social revolution. A Marxist analysis suggests the following about the unstable role of criminals who remain lumpen, without a political consciousness:

> They can be courageous fighters against the bourgeoisie and the state, but their tendency is to reject the leadership of the proletariat, to reject the discipline and study necessary for a long protracted struggle to overthrow capitalism and institute socialism, to fail to see the necessity of winning over the masses, to fail to clearly distinguish friends from enemies, to advocate adventurous tactics, to adopt destructive and "roving rebel" tactics, and to seek personal glory and power. While there are many negative tendencies among the lumpen, their hatred of the system and courage in fighting it should not be ignored. If led by a strong and disciplined proletarian revolutionary movement, elements of the lumpen can become courageous allies of the working class.[70]

The problem is that of developing a revolutionary consciousness among those who resist capitalist conditions.

The task of a Marxist criminology is to develop a political consciousness among all people who are oppressed by the

70. Hill, *Class Analysis,* pp. 86–87.

capitalist system. This work is engaged in daily in a multitude of ways: as we attempt to break the conventional ideology of criminal reality, as we investigate the conditions for the development of political consciousness and revolutionary actions, as we participate in criminal justice workplace activity, as we are part of the prisoners' movement, and as we create new forms of political work and consciousness among ourselves.

Our project is to turn the social action under capitalism into revolutionary activity. As politically conscious activity, criminally defined actions against capitalism thus cease to negate themselves. Instead of criminality being unconscious reaction–often against members of one's own class–actions are directed against the capitalist system. The act of revolt thus acquires its subversive quality and becomes invested with its full potential. Social action rather than affirming bourgeois values, by being reabsorbed into the source of its creation, goes outside the system of oppression to become a revolutionary act. Politically conscious action in such fashion becomes an inevitable part of the class struggle in capitalist society.

4

THE POLITICAL ECONOMY OF CRIMINAL JUSTICE

The capitalist state promotes the further development of the capitalist mode of production. The state, under late capitalism, must establish the general framework for capital accumulation and foster the conditions for maintaining the capitalist system. In assuring capital accumulation, exploitative social relations are reproduced and even heightened. The social problems generated by the capitalist system are increased with the further development of capitalism.

The class struggle under late capitalism must be regulated by the state. The repressive apparatus of the state becomes ever more important in the development of capitalism. Policies of control–especially crime control–are instituted in the attempt to regulate problems and conflicts that otherwise can be solved only by social and economic changes that go beyond capitalist reforms. Criminal justice, as the euphemism for controlling class struggle and administering legal repression, becomes a major type of social policy in the advanced stages of capitalism.

Emerging within the political economy of late capitalism is a political economy of criminal justice. The political economy of criminal justice is one of the fundamental characteristics of advanced capitalism. To understand its various features is to understand a crucial part of the capitalist system. Criminal justice will likely increase as a capitalist response to the contradictions of late capitalism.

STATE EXPENDITURE ON CRIMINAL JUSTICE

The capitalist state must increasingly expend its resources on programs that secure the capitalist order. These *social expenses* of the state, as defined by James O'Connor, consist of "projects and services which are required to maintain social harmony–to fulfill the state's 'legitimization' function." [1] While *social capital* is expended in the promotion of profitable private accumulation, the social expenses of the state are not directly productive, producing no surplus value. They are designed to keep "social peace" among unemployed workers, or among the surplus population in general. Welfare and law enforcement are the primary forms of the state's social expenses, regulating class struggle, repressing action against the existing order, and giving legitimacy to the capitalist system. The creation and administration of the criminal justice system as a whole has become a principal social expense of the capitalist state.

The state in promoting capital accumulation in the monopoly sector stimulates overproduction and thereby creates a surplus population and the resulting need for state ex-

1. James O'Connor, *The Fiscal Crisis of the State* (New York: St. Martin's Press, 1973), p. 7.

penses to cope with the surplus population. Such social services as education, family support, health services, and housing benefits give legitimacy to the capitalist system and satisfy some of the needs of the working class. These services compensate in part for the oppression and suffering caused by capitalism.[2]

The criminal justice system, on the other hand, serves more explicitly to control that which cannot be remedied by available employment within the economy or by social services for the surplus population. The police, the courts, and the penal agencies–the entire criminal justice system –expands to cope as a last resort with the problems of surplus population. As the contradictions of capitalism increase, the criminal justice system becomes a preventive institution as well as a control and corrective agency. State expenditures on criminal justice occupy a larger share of the state's budgetary expenses. Criminal justice as a social expense of the state necessarily expands with the further development of capitalism.

Since the declaration of the war on crime in the mid-1960s, the amount of money spent on criminal justice has climbed steadily. The federal government, as only one portion of the state apparatus, has increased its budgetary outlays from less than one-half billion dollars in 1967 to nearly $3.5 billion in 1977 (see figure 2). These increased federal expenditures are for the federal government's enforcement and prosecution efforts, but are also for the assistance of law-enforcement and judicial activities of state and local governments.

With the passage of the Omnibus Crime Control and Safe Streets Act and the establishment of the Law Enforcement Assistance Administration (LEAA), the federal gov-

2. See Ian Gough, "State Expenditure in Advanced Capitalism," *New Left Review,* no. 92 (July–August 1975): esp. 70–74.

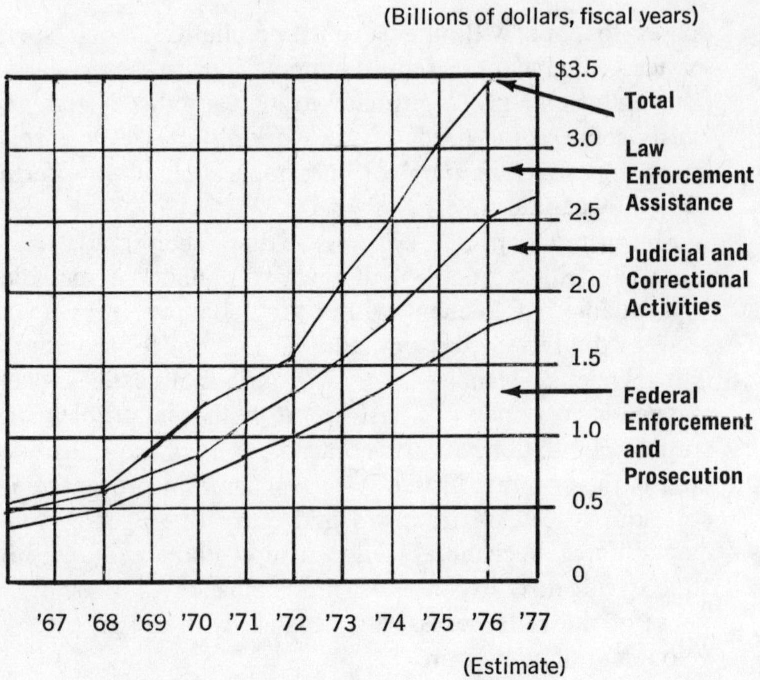

(Billions of dollars, fiscal years)

$3.5
3.0
2.5
2.0
1.5
1.0
0.5
0

Total

Law Enforcement Assistance

Judicial and Correctional Activities

Federal Enforcement and Prosecution

'67 '68 '69 '70 '71 '72 '73 '74 '75 '76 '77

(Estimate)

FIGURE 2. FEDERAL EXPENDITURES ON CRIMINAL JUSTICE, 1967–77

Source: Office of Management and Budget.

ernment has created a new level of crime control, providing a broader and more pervasive organization of criminal justice. The mission of the newly created LEAA was stated clearly at the beginning:

> The mission of LEAA is to reduce crime and delinquency by channeling Federal financial aid to state and local governments, to conduct research in methods of improving law enforcement and criminal justice, to fund efforts to upgrade the educational level of law enforcement personnel, to develop applications of statistical research and applied systems analysis in law enforcement, and to develop broad policy guidelines for both the short and long-range improvement of the nation's Criminal Justice System as a whole.[3]

The budget of LEAA, as one portion of federal expenditures on criminal justice, has grown sharply from a first-year expenditure in 1969 of $60 million to $880 million in 1977. The major part of LEAA's budget goes to states and localities for the improvement of criminal justice activities and for the development of new techniques of control. In addition, funds are provided for training law-enforcement agents and for research on improving criminal justice. The accomplishments of LEAA, working "in partnership with the states and localities in improving the criminal justice system and reducing crime," are described as follows:

> –The states have received nearly $2 billion in block action grants and $371 million in corrections money. These grants have funded more than 60,000 projects.
> –The states have received $201 million in planning

3. Law Enforcement Assistance Administration, *3rd Annual Report of the Law Enforcement Assistance Administration, Fiscal Year 1971* (Washington, D.C.: U.S. Government Printing Office, 1972), p. ii.

funds to develop comprehensive, detailed plans on how they intend to reduce and prevent crime.

–Approximately 200,000 students have received $150 million in Law Enforcement Education Program funds to finance studies for law enforcement and criminal justice careers.

–The National Institute of Law Enforcement and Criminal Justice, LEAA's research arm, has invested more than $110 million in research and development projects.

–LEAA's National Criminal Justice Information and Statistics Service has committed approximately $38.5 million to statistical studies to draw a better picture of crime in the United States, the number of jails and prisons, and a wealth of other information never before available.[4]

In spite of the diverse categories of funding, about half the money is actually spent on law-enforcement operations. The result is a coordinated system of legal repression for the advanced capitalist society. For the first time in the history of the United States, all levels of the state and the various agencies of the law are linked together in a nationwide system of criminal justice.

The federal expenditures on criminal justice are aimed in two directions. There are the *direct expenditures* (including cost of salaries, materials, supplies, contractual services, plus capital outlay) that finance the federal government's criminal justice activities. But growing in importance as the federal government designs and supports a nationwide criminal justice system are the *intergovernmental expendi-*

4. Law Enforcement Assistance Administration, *Sixth Annual Report of LEAA, Fiscal Year 1974* (Washington, D.C.: U.S. Government Printing Office, 1974), p. 4.

tures, which consist of grants, shared revenues, and the cost of services the federal government provides for state and local governments. A major portion of federal spending on criminal justice in recent years has been on intergovernmental expenditures. Federal intergovernmental expenditures rose from $237 million in 1971 (of a total federal expenditure of $1.5 billion) to $642 million in 1974 (of a total federal expenditure of $2.6 billion).[5] Virtually all the increase is attributable to the expanding programs of LEAA that distributed hundreds of millions of dollars to state and local governments.

The *total expenditure* for criminal justice by the capitalist state, for *all* levels of government, is considerable. In the fiscal year 1974 nearly $15 billion was spent on criminal justice in the United States.[6] As shown in table 2, well over half this expenditure ($8.5 billion) was on law enforcement. The next largest amount ($3.2 billion) was spent on the correctional system.

Of the various levels of government, the largest expenditures for criminal justice are made by the state and local governments. Local governments spend more for all criminal justice activities than federal and state governments combined. In the fiscal year 1974, of a total criminal justice expenditure of nearly $15 billion for all levels of government: the federal government spent $2.6 billion and the state governments spent $4.5 billion, while the expenditure by the local governments amounted to $9.1 billion for criminal justice. When each type of criminal justice activity is examined separately for each level of government, it be-

5. National Criminal Justice Information and Statistics Service, *Expenditure and Employment Data for the Criminal Justice System, 1974* (Washington, D.C.: U.S. Government Printing Office, 1976), p. 21.
6. Ibid.

TABLE 2. GOVERNMENT EXPENDITURE FOR CRIMINAL JUSTICE FISCAL YEAR 1974
(Dollar amounts in thousands)

Criminal Justice Activity	All Governments	Federal Government	State Government	Local Governments
Total criminal justice activity	$14,953,661	$2,602,958	$4,546,345	$9,129,864
Police protection	8,511,676	1,224,586	1,382,931	5,984,077
Judicial	1,798,153	136,135	475,992	1,227,391
Legal services and prosecution	770,762	117,798	181,537	476,793
Indigent defense	244,593	91,629	58,055	101,445
Corrections	3,240,396	237,300	1,895,434	1,240,815
Other criminal justice	388,081	795,510	552,396	99,343

Source: National Criminal Justice Information and Statistics Service, *Expenditure and Employment Data for the Criminal Justice System, 1974* (Washington, D.C.: U.S. Government Printing Office, 1976), p. 21.

comes clear that the different levels of government concentrate their crime control efforts on particular areas of criminal justice. As shown in table 2, the local governments support the police and the courts, involving the arrest and prosecution of cases; the state expenditures go mainly for the punishment and correction of offenders, with some attention to criminal justice planning and the formation of new criminal justice programs and agencies; and half the federal government's expenditures are for law enforcement, including funds to support state and local law enforcement.

The largest share of criminal justice system expenditures is obviously spent on the *employment* of workers within the system. In recent years the number of criminal justice employees has increased to over one million persons working in the criminal justice system in the United States. According to the statistics for the year 1974, 95,252 of these workers are employed by the federal government, 262,735

TABLE 3. EMPLOYMENT FOR THE CRIMINAL JUSTICE SYSTEM, BY LEVEL OF GOVERNMENT, 1974

Criminal Justice Activity	All Governments	Federal Government	State Governments	Local Governments
Total criminal justice system	1,093,609	95,252	262,735	735,622
Police protection	653,580	69,420	97,224	486,936
Judicial	141,094	6,804	24,560	109,730
Legal services and prosecution	58,582	7,091	12,381	39,110
Indigent defense	6,687	154	2,710	3,823
Corrections	226,794	10,126	122,560	94,108
Other criminal justice	6,872	1,657	3,300	1,915

Source: National Criminal Justice Information and Statistics Service, *Expenditure and Employment Data for the Criminal Justice System, 1974* (Washington, D.C.: U.S. Government Printing Office, 1976), p. 21.

by state governments, and 735,622 by local governments.[7] In terms of proportions, 67.3 percent of the criminal justice employees are employed by local governments, 24.0 by state governments, and 8.7 by the federal government. The employee figures for the various criminal justice activities, by level of government, are in table 3. Moreover, the fact that the payroll for all criminal justice employees in the United States amounts to over one billion dollars each month, means that about 80 percent of criminal justice expenditures are for the employment of criminal justice workers. That the criminal justice system is built on the labors of the class that is itself the object of criminal justice is a point not to be missed in understanding the political economy of criminal justice.

Workers in the criminal justice system, then, provide in their labor "the use-value of ensuring the maintenance of

7. Ibid.

the capitalist class structure."[8] They are the "repressive workers" in that they engage in the actual or threatened use of physical force and legal punishment. While they do not produce surplus value, they do secure the social order (through the apparatus of the capitalist state) so that capitalists can privately accumulate capital. The concrete use-value of their work is to maintain domestic order, to make the society safe for capitalist accumulation and to protect class relations. Although these workers occupy a fraction within the working class, and are not therefore members of the "ruling class," in terms of the use-value of their labor they act against their own working-class interests. This contradiction obscures their class struggle and at the same time provokes a tension that undermines the possibility of continued repression by the capitalist state.

Beyond the contradiction of criminal justice work is the long-term problem of financing the entire criminal justice system. The purpose of the criminal justice system is that of maintaining *social peace*. State expenditure on criminal justice does not directly contribute to the accumulation of private capital and the creation of surplus value. Rather, the criminal justice system secures the capitalist order so that the capitalist class can continue to accumulate capital. The crisis, however, becomes a fiscal one: state expenditures on criminal justice grow faster than the revenues available to support an expanding criminal justice system.[9] Yet, as the social problems generated by the capitalist mode of production grow, repressive measures must be expanded.

8. Francesca Freedman, "The Internal Structure of the American Proletariat: A Marxist Analysis," *Socialist Revolution* 5 (October–December 1975): 73. Also see James O'Connor's discussion of "guard labor" in his article "Productive and Unproductive Labor," *Politics and Society* 5, no. 3 (1975): 297–336.
9. On the fiscal crisis of legitimation functions in general, see O'Connor, *Fiscal Crisis of the State,* esp. pp. 150–178.

Criminal justice is a social expense that the capitalist state must continue to finance in order to promote the social order of advanced capitalism.

The late capitalist economy cannot be secured solely by a repressive state, however. Legitimacy has to be restored in ways that are less obviously repressive. But restoration seems unlikely at this stage of class struggle in the development of capitalism. Embedded in crisis and contradiction, the criminal justice system as a last resort signals the imminent demise of the capitalist state and the capitalist mode of production. The concrete political practice for the working class emerges at this point in capitalism.

THE CRIMINAL JUSTICE–INDUSTRIAL COMPLEX

The state, in its efforts to stimulate capital accumulation and stabilize the social order, forms an alliance with the monopoly sector of the economy. The monopoly sector, which consists of the large corporations and multinationals that control virtually all capital-intensive industries, is the primary force of private capital accumulation in the advanced capitalist economy. The continued growth of the monopoly sector becomes increasingly dependent on the state. In a symbiotic relationship, the continued growth of the state depends on the expansion of the monopoly sector. The state provides the structure for the economic development of the monopoly sector; and the state, in turn, depends on the monopoly sector for its economic well-being as well as the services and technology for maintaining social stability.

Hence, a "social-industrial complex" has emerged, an involvement of industry in the planning, production, and operation of state programs.[10] These state-financed pro-

10. Ibid., pp. 51–58.

grams (centered around education, welfare, and criminal justice), as social expenses necessary for maintaining social order, are furnished by monopoly industries. The industries develop programs that simultaneously secure the social order for the state and improve the productivity and profitability of the industries themselves, while attempting to make a safe environment for continued capitalist development. As a consequence of the new social-industrial complex, monopoly capital has a new source from which to gain profits. Social programs financed by the state provide new investment opportunities for monopoly industries. As noted in the business community: "Companies from AT&T to Xerox have been urged to–and in many cases have willingly accepted–the challenges to educate our children, police our streets, clean up our polluted air and water, teach our disadvantaged citizens how to earn a living, rebuild our slums, and even tell us how to run our cities more efficiently." [11] A new growth industry is thus being sponsored by the state, for the mutual benefit of both the state and monopoly capital–for the intended survival of the capitalist system.

A major part of the new and growing social-industrial complex is what we can call the "criminal justice–industrial complex." Criminal justice, in all its aspects, is becoming one of the last remaining capital-investment industries. That industry finds it profitable to invest in crime is one of the final contradictions of the capitalist system.

The criminal justice–industrial complex has grown steadily since the mid-1960s, when the state elevated social control to a "war on crime." In the process, a technocratic solution to social disorder has emerged in which a new and

11. "Should Business Tackle Society's Problems?" in *Economic and Business News* (Boston: Houghton Mifflin, 1972), p. 3. Quoted in O'Connor, *Fiscal Crisis of the State,* p. 55.

profitable alliance has been formed between the state and monopoly industries in the control of the domestic population. Contained in the special task force report on *Science and Technology,* completed for the President's Commission on Law Enforcement and Administration of Justice, was the explicit message that (1) crime control must become more scientific; (2) crime control must utilize the kind of science and technology that already serves the military; and (3) the federal government must institute and support such a program, with the assistance of private industry.[12] That a science and technology could be developed, similar to that of the military, was the good news presented in the opening lines of the task force report:

> The natural sciences and technology have long helped the police to solve specific crimes. Scientists and engineers have had very little impact, however, on the overall operations of the criminal justice system and its principal components: police, courts, and corrections. More than 200,000 scientists and engineers have applied themselves to solving military problems and hundreds of thousands more to innovation in other areas of modern life, but only a handful are working to control the crimes that injure or frighten millions of Americans each year. Yet, the two communities have much to offer each other: science and technology is a valuable source of knowledge and techniques for combating crime; the criminal justice system represents a vast area of challenging problems.[13]

The kinds of equipment and tactics needed for the criminal justice system were then noted:

12. President's Commission on Law Enforcement and Administration of Justice, *Science and Technology, Task Force Report,* prepared by the Institute for Defense Analyses (Washington, D.C.: U.S. Government Printing Office, 1967).
13. Ibid., p. 1.

> In the traditional view, science and technology primarily means new equipment. And modern technology can, indeed, provide a vast array of devices beyond those now in general use to improve the operations of criminal justice agencies, particularly in helping the police deter crime and apprehend criminals. Some of the more important possibilities are:
>
> –Electronic computers for processing the enormous quantities of needed data.
> –Police radio networks connecting officers and neighboring departments.
> –Inexpensive, light two-way portable radios for every patrolman.
> –Computers for processing fingerprints.
> –Instruments for identifying criminals by their voice, photographs, hair, blood, body chemistry, etc.
> –Devices for automatic and continual reporting of all police car locations.
> –Helicopters for airborne police patrol.
> –Inexpensive, reliable burglar and robbery alarms.
> –Nonlethal weapons to subdue dangerous criminals without inflicting permanent harm.
> –Perimeter surveillance devices for prisoners.
> –Automatic transcription devices for courtroom testimony. Many of these devices are now in existence, some as prototypes and some available commercially. Others still require basic development but are at least technically feasible and worthy of further exploration.[14]

The new technocratic approach to crime and social control has developed rapidly in the last decade. Especially under the direction of LEAA, a multimillion-dollar market in domestic control has been established for hundreds of industries and research institutes.[15] LEAA has contracted

14. Ibid.
15. Gregory McLauchlan, "LEAA: A Case Study in the Development of the Social Industrial Complex," *Crime and Social Justice* 4 (Fall–Winter 1975): 15–23.

industries and institutes, directly or indirectly through state agencies, to develop and manufacture a wide range of weapons and technical devices for use in the criminal justice system. A technology and an industry created for scientific warfare abroad is now being applied to social control at home. Moreover, a field of research and development in criminal justice has emerged, putting control on a scientific basis as well as making a profitable industry. Under the sponsorship of LEAA, with lucrative contracts, private corporations, research institutes, and universities are gaining profits from the new system of criminal justice.

In fact, the political and economic meaning of LEAA in the development of the criminal justice–industrial complex is now clear. As shown by Gregory McLauchlan, LEAA is simultaneously directing the technocratic solution to social control, guiding the development of a social-industrial complex in criminal justice, *and* lowering the social expense of criminal justice by making social expenditures profitable for private industry. LEAA is thus attempting to reverse the economic burden, and possible crisis, of the social expense of controlling crime. In summarizing this observation, McLauchlan writes:

> LEAA represents a federal infrastructure which attempts to simultaneously rationalize the fiscal crisis of state finance, and develop a social-industrial complex in the field of law enforcement. By providing rationalized and efficient standards of organization for a nationally-integrated law enforcement apparatus, LEAA can reduce social expenses over the long run. Presently, most state expenditure on law enforcement consists of social expenses (i.e., administrative costs and salaries) which do not increase productivity or reduce the cost of reproducing the labor force. However, LEAA is attempting to reverse this tendency by increasing expenditures on sophisticated technology and hardware for

police operations. In so doing, the labor-to-capital ratio of law enforcement programs will be reduced, thus lowering social expenses.[16]

The criminal justice–industrial complex thus becomes visible as a structure in which capital accumulation is being combined with the social expenditure of the state. The growth of state spending on social programs is joined under advanced capitalism with the growth of the monopoly sector. The contradiction is that while the purpose of state-financed social programs is to legitimate the existing order, the collusion between the state and monopoly industries weakens the legitimacy of the capitalist system. In the long run, in the course of continued class struggle, the criminal justice–industrial complex cannot be a lasting solution to the joint problems of capital accumulation and social stability.

Nevertheless, because of limited alternatives within the capitalist framework, the criminal justice–industrial complex continues to grow. As the expenditures for criminal justice expand, the involvement of the monopoly sector increases. Private industries are not only increasingly engaged in the development and manufacture of the hardware for law enforcement (including guns, ammunition, gas, helmets, helicopters, electronic detection devices, communications equipment, and the like), but they develop and manufacture more sophisticated and subtle forms of control technology. The state in collaboration with private industry now plans and implements technocratic solutions to crime control that include systems analysis, managerial improvement, computerized intelligence surveillance, and administrative reorganization. Criminal justice administration becomes modeled on the corporate form, while the

16. Ibid., p. 21.

tactical operations are borrowed from the military.[17] This corporate-military approach to criminal justice meets the requirements of controlling the domestic population under advanced capitalism and readily engages monopoly capital in the state's program of criminal justice.

Added to the criminal justice–industrial complex, and increasing in importance, is the direct involvement of the private sector itself in crime control. Although we continue to believe that criminal justice is the sole province of the state, the fact is that private industry is engaged in aspects of criminal justice, especially law enforcement. The private security industry, in particular, is growing steadily each year. Expenditures on uniformed guards and private detective services amounts to about $15 million a year.[18] And, contrary to common knowledge, private police outnumber public police in most cities and states in the United States. The benefits to private industry are contradictory, however. On the one hand, private policing is obviously beneficial to the private policy industry. But for the rest of private industry, the costs of private law enforcement take away from profits. This is a case of private industry in conflict with itself. The capitalist mode of production is reaching a point where the problems it generates cannot be adequately met by either the private sector, the state sector, or the private and state sector in collaboration.

As the crisis of the state and the capitalist economy accelerates, forms of control will be devised that attempt to be more pervasive and more certain and, at the same time, less of an expense for the state. The state and monopoly

17. Center for Research on Criminal Justice, *The Iron Fist and the Velvet Glove: An Analysis of the U.S. Police* (Berkeley, Calif.: Center for Research on Criminal Justice, 1975), pp. 32–37.
18. Michael T. Klare, "The Boom in Private Police," *Nation* 221 (15 November 1975): 486–91.

capital will try to create crime control programs that do not require a major outlay of capital, capital that does not promote further capital accumulation. For example, halfway-house programs may in some cases be substituted for large and costly institutions. Surveillance may replace some other forms of confinement and control. Yet the contradiction is only furthered: criminal justice is inevitably a losing battle under late capitalism.

In other words, criminal justice spending is only a partial, temporary, and self-defeating resolution to capitalist economic contradictions. The situation is similar to military spending. While expenditures on warfare and the military may have some immediate functions for the state and the economy, an economy based on such expenditure is subject to more contradictions than ultimate resolutions.[19] A substantial criminal justice budget, similar to a military budget, cannot successfully solve the economic and political problems of the capitalist system. And in the long run, criminal justice as a social expenditure can only further the contradictions of capitalism.

ECONOMIC COSTS OF CRIME

Given the inherent contradictions of social expenditures on criminal justice, the only framework within which criminal justice policy can operate is that of the relative *costs* of crime in capitalist society. Rather than solving the crime problem, the question becomes one of determining how much crime the society can afford. The costs are usually considered in terms of the "direct costs," attributable to the

19. Clarence Y. H. Lo, "The Conflicting Functions of U.S. Military Spending after World War II," *Kapitalistate*, no. 3 (Spring 1975): 26–44.

offenses themselves (including money lost and lives taken), and the "indirect costs," attributable to the control of crime (the expense of running the criminal justice system).[20] The problem, then, is to determine the direct and indirect costs of the amount and kinds of crime generated in the society.

The orthodox economist wants to know what it would cost to reduce crime, striking some balance between the costs resulting from crime and the costs of preventing that crime. Such analysis is guided by a "cost-benefit" calculation. The purpose is to furnish knowledge necessary for policies for controlling and preventing crime: "By using methods such as cost-benefit analysis, systems analysis, and program budgeting, economists are striving to develop criteria for an improved allocation of resources in law enforcement. For research purposes the economists assume that all divisions of the criminal justice have one goal: the protection of society."[21] The conventional economic analysis of crime is a science for preserving the social order of advanced capitalism.

The conventional economic analysis of crime also assumes the functional inevitability of crime. In viewing crime in functional terms, this kind of analysis leads to the absurd position of seeing crime as a necessary feature of society.[22] Such analysis thus supports theories and practices aimed solely at the control of criminals, rather than at the pathology of the capitalist system. This type of analysis, as noted in a critique, can never get at the underlying causes of crime: "The fight against criminality can therefore no

20. John E. Conklin, *The Impact of Crime* (New York: Macmillan, 1975), pp. 1–14.
21. Richard F. Sullivan, "The Economics of Crime: An Introduction to the Literature," *Crime and Delinquency* 19 (April 1973): 138.
22. For a critique, see Ian Taylor, Paul Walton, and Jock Young, *The New Criminology: For a Social Theory of Deviance* (New York: Harper & Row, 1973), pp. 212–21.

longer mean a fight against the causes of criminality because it is futile to fight against 'inevitable' conditions; instead the problem becomes one of making the means of social control more effective, since they are then the only means of containing the *extent* of criminality."[23] By focusing on the conditions that complicate or enhance effective crime control, the pathologies of the society are ignored and the existing order is supported. A Marxist analysis of crime, in contrast, assumes that there is a social order in which crime is not inevitable.

But given the nature of capitalism, the fact is that crime has become an integral part of capitalist society. Crime in the United States, in an irrational and ironical way, is a "normal" part of society. A capitalist economy based on exploitation and oppression generates a crime problem that can be "solved" only by controlling that problem. Only by going beyond capitalism, to socialism, could the contradictions that produce the crime problem be confronted. Crime will continue to be "inevitable" as long as a capitalist society exists.

The economic costs, and irrational functions, of crime are readily apparent in the economy of the United States. The "direct" costs are usually measured in terms of number of offenses and the amount of dollars lost. For example, according to the official statistics of the crimes reported to the police in 1975, 464,973 people were robbed; 3,252,129 people had their homes or businesses burglarized; there were 5,977,698 cases of larceny; and 1,000,455 automobiles were stolen.[24] The reported dollar loss for

23. Falco Werkentin, Michael Hofferbert, and Michael Baurmann, Criminology as Police Science or: 'How Old is the New Criminology?' " *Crime and Social Justice* 2 (Fall–Winter 1974): 28.

24. Federal Bureau of Investigation, *Uniform Crime Reports, 1975* (Washington, D.C.: U.S. Government Printing Office, 1976), pp. 10–49.

robbery amounted to $154 million; $1.4 billion was lost through burglary; and the loss for the victims of larceny was $992 million. All the rates for these offenses have increased in recent years (from 1970 to 1975), with robbery up 27 percent, burglary up 41 percent, and larceny up 35 percent. The economic costs of the traditional crimes continue to increase in the late stage of advanced capitalism.

This only begins to touch the surface of the "direct" costs of crime. For instance, in the case of the traditional offenses of robbery, burglary, and larceny, only a portion of the offenses are ever reported to the police, greatly underestimating the actual number of crimes. When victimization survey statistics are used, the rates of crime turn out to be much higher than those resulting from reports to the police. Taking the victimization for one city, for example, in New York 47 percent of all robberies are reported to the police; 52 percent of burglaries; and only 33 percent of larcenies.[25] The dollar loss of the offenses that go unreported to the police certainly raise the total economic cost of crime.

Added to these costs are the billions of dollars that are taken or lost through such offenses as embezzlement, fraud, extortion, tax violations, forgery, and vandalism. Beyond the costs of these offenses are the losses due to the crimes of the government, the capitalists, and the corporations against the rest of the population. These offenses take a daily economic toll that is beyond estimation. For example, there are the losses due to sickness and death resulting from pollution of food and environment; disabilities from industrial accidents; injuries from police brutality; and the loss of jobs and income through unemployment, racism, and sexism. With these offenses there are economic costs that go

25. Law Enforcement Assistance Administration, *Sixth Annual Report of LEAA,* p. 208.

far beyond the direct loss of money taken. There is the question of life itself.

The "indirect" costs of crime have already been indicated, mainly as the social expenditure for criminal justice. The cost of maintaining the expanding criminal system increases each year. About $15 billion is currently being spent annually by the government on the police, the courts, and corrections. Added to the government expenditures on criminal justice are the private expenditures, especially the $10 to $15 billion spent yearly on the private police. Not possible of measurement are the economic costs that individuals, groups, and governments pay and suffer from the existence of crime in the society. A society and economy without the kinds and amounts of crime found under capitalism would be much different from what we know in the United States. Since crime is such a pervasive part of the economy in the United States, an exact determination of its costs and benefits are impossible as well as an absurd undertaking.

In the course of briefly discussing crime, Marx pointed out ironically the ways in which crime is "productive" in capitalist society. For instance, Marx wrote, the criminal "produces the whole of the police and of criminal justice, constables, judges, hangmen, juries, etc.; and all these different lines of business, which form equally many categories of the social division of labor, develop different capacities of the human spirit, create new needs and new ways of satisfying them."[26] Only in a very irrational way, and within an absurd functional reasoning, does crime contribute to capitalist society.

> The criminal breaks the monotony and everyday security of bourgeois life. In this way he keeps it from stagnation, and

26. Karl Marx, *Theories of Surplus-Value*, pt. 1 (Moscow: Progress Publishers, 1963), p. 387.

> gives rise to that uneasy tension and agility without which even the spur of competition would get blunted. Thus he gives a stimulus to the productive forces. While crime takes a part of the superfluous population off the labor market and thus reduces competition among the laborers–up to a certain point preventing wages from falling below the minimum–the struggle against crime absorbs another part of this population. Thus the criminal comes in as one of those natural "counterweights" which bring about a correct balance and open up a whole perspective of "useful" occupations.[27]

But, as Marx indicated, crime is by no means necessary for society. Yet under capitalism even crime seems to play a part in a social order that is pathological in its very nature.

While it is true that hundreds of thousands of people find employment in fighting crime and hundreds of thousands find economic support through criminal offenses and economic security while being confined in prison, at the same time lowering the unemployment rate of the society, this does not mean that crime is necessary and inevitable. It means that under capitalism crime is generated within the capitalist mode of production. However, in no long-term way can crime be functional even within capitalism. It results from the contradictions of capitalism, and it contributes further to these contradictions.

The capitalist class recognizes the high cost of crime. The corporate world is concerned and alarmed about the economic costs of crime. In a study made in 1974 by the Economic Unit of *U.S. News & World Report,* the "high price tag" of crime was dramatized.[28] The magazine estimated the economic cost of crime to be nearly $90 billion,

27. Ibid., pp. 387–88.
28. "The Losing Battle Against Crime in America," *U.S. News & World Report,* 16 December 1974, pp. 30–40.

an increase of 73.4 percent since a study made four years earlier. Even in an era of rising prices, as *U.S. News & World Report* observed, this is "frightening inflation." The sense of alarm in the corporate world is noted in an opening statement of the magazine's report:

> Almost everywhere you look–and in almost every type of crime–the picture is getting grimmer. Youngsters are becoming criminals in soaring numbers, and turning rapidly from "kid stuff" to major violence.
>
> Crooked business executives and thieving employes are swelling the cost of "white collar" crime. Economic hard times are spurring a rise in burglary and theft. "Career criminals" go in and out of jail as though through a revolving door, finding so little risk they keep repeating their offenses. The Federal Government is winning more battles–but has not yet won the war–against organized crime. Terrorism–by kidnapers, bombers and extortionists–is spreading.
>
> No part of the nation is safe any more, as crime skyrockets in small towns and suburbs. The following reports, from "U.S. News & World Report" staff members and bureaus in all parts of the country, show the enormity of the crime problem confronting this nation–and the lack of any real solutions.[29]

Certainly there is no solution within the capitalist framework.

To reduce crime and thereby reduce the economic costs of crime would be to change beyond recognition the capitalist system. Crime in all its aspects, with all its economic costs, is the price the capitalist system pays for capitalism. Unfortunately, it is a price we all pay. The economic costs of crime become an issue–but go beyond conventional

29. Ibid., p. 33.

calls for more criminal justice—in the struggle for a socialist society.

CONTROL OF SURPLUS POPULATION

Social expenditures on criminal justice necessarily increase with the development of advanced capitalism. In the late stages of capitalism the mode of production and the forms of capital accumulation accelerate the growth of the relative surplus population. The state must then provide social expense programs, including criminal justice, both to legitimate advanced capitalism and to control the surplus population. Rather than being capable of absorbing the surplus population into the political economy, advanced capitalism can only supervise and control a population that is now superfluous to the capitalist system. The problem is especially acute when the surplus population threatens to disturb the system, either by overburdening the system or by political action. Criminal justice is the modern means of controlling this surplus population produced by late capitalist development.

The state attempts to offset the social expense of criminal justice by supporting the growth of the criminal justice–industrial complex. The fiscal crisis of the capitalist state is temporarily alleviated by forming an alliance between monopoly capital and state-financed social programs. The social programs of the state are thereby transformed into social capital, providing subsidized investment opportunities for monopoly capital and ameliorating some of the material impoverishment of the surplus population.[30] The new complex thus ties the surplus population to the state and to the political economy of advanced capitalism. While a

30. O'Connor, *Fiscal Crisis of the State,* p. 221.

growing segment of the population is absorbed into the system as *indirectly productive workers*–the army of government and office workers, paraprofessionals, and those who work in one way or another in the social expense programs–there is also a large surplus population that is controlled by these programs. These unemployed, underemployed, reserve army workers now find themselves dependent on the state. They are linked to the state (and to monopoly capital) for much of their economic welfare, and they are linked in being the object of the social control programs of the state. The criminal justice system is the most explicit of these programs in controlling the surplus population. Criminal justice and the surplus population are thus symbiotically interdependent.

As the surplus population grows with the development of capitalism, the criminal justice system or some equivalent must also grow. An expanding criminal justice system is the only way late capitalism can "integrate" the surplus population into the overall economic and political system. The notion that the social problems generated by capitalism can be solved becomes obsolete. Instead, problems such as crime are dealt with in terms of a *control* model. When the underlying conditions of capitalism cannot be changed–without changing the capitalist system itself–controlling the population oppressed by the existing conditions is the only "solution." Thus as one theorist-strategist of the capitalist state puts it, we must "learn to live with crime"; and the important question then becomes "what constitutes an effective law-enforcement and order-maintenance system?" [31]

On all levels of the criminal justice system new tech-

31. James Q. Wilson, "Crime and Law Enforcement," in *Agenda for the Nation,* ed. Kermit Gordon (Washington, D.C.: U.S. Government Printing Office), pp. 199 and 204.

niques of control are being developed and instituted. Not only has there been increased implementation of a military-hardware approach to criminal justice, but developing more recently alongside are more subtle approaches. A dual system is developing whereby some actions of the surplus population that are defined as criminal are dealt with harshly by strong-arm techniques and by punitive measures. Other actions by other portions of the surplus population are handled by such software techniques as diversion from the courts and community-based corrections. In general, however, whatever the current techniques, the new model is one of *pacification*. The surplus population is not only to be controlled, but it is to accept this control. As the authors of *The Iron Fist and the Velvet Glove* note, in regard to the law-enforcement aspects of the criminal justice system, the system is developing as follows:

> During the late 1960s, the technical and managerial approach to police work represented by the military-corporate model came under increasing criticism. More sophisticated analyses of crime and urban disorder suggested that massive spending on military hardware, by itself, would not only fail to stop rising crime rates and urban discontent, but would probably serve to further alienate large sectors of the population. This approach stressed the need for the police to develop closer ties to the communities most heavily patrolled by them. The emphasis began to be placed less on paramilitary efficiency and more on insuring popular consent and acquiescence. The idea that police departments should engage in some sort of "community relations" had, of course, been around for some time, but community relations programs, in practice, were few, and those that did exist were generally regarded as ineffective window-dressing. The new emphasis, on the other hand, represented a serious attempt to supplement the growing technological prowess of the police

> with programs that could make the police role more acceptable to the people most affected by it.[32]

The capitalist state, in alliance with monopoly capital, must continually innovate in expanding the criminal justice system.

Whatever the techniques of control, the fact remains that it is the surplus population that is in need of control, that is being controlled by the criminal justice system. Control is especially acute in those periods when the economic crisis is most obvious—during periods of depression and recession. It is during these times that the surplus population is affected most; and it is during these times that the surplus population grows through unemployment.

As usual during these periods, the hardest-hit groups are women, blacks, the young, and unskilled workers. For example, in 1974 the unemployment rate among nonwhites was twice as high as that of whites; almost half the unemployed were women, although they occupied only about 40 percent of the labor force; the unemployment rate of young workers (16–21 years) was twice the average rate of workers; and the unemployment rate of unskilled workers was several percentage points higher than that for all other workers.[33] Moreover, these figures drastically underestimate the extent of unemployment in the United States. While the official statistics indicated that 5 million people were unemployed in 1974, this figure obscures the fact that over 18 million people were out of work at some time during the year. In 1975 nearly 24 million people were unemployed at some time during the year, a figure representing one out of every four workers.

32. Center for Research on Criminal Justice, *The Iron Fist and the Velvet Glove,* p. 54.
33. "Unemployment Stays High," *Dollars & Sense,* no. 13 (January 1976): 10–11.

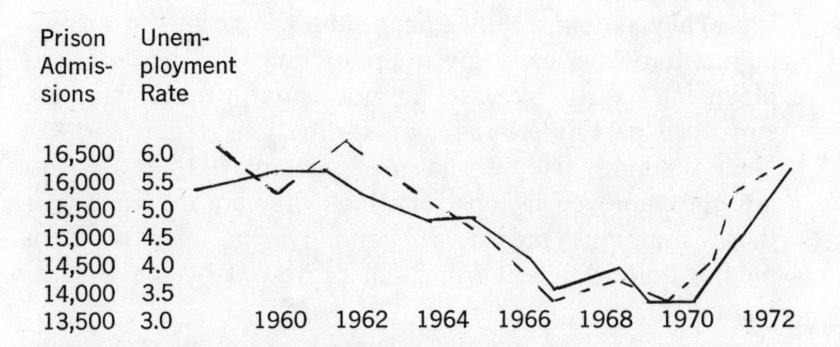

FIGURE 3. PRISONS AND UNEMPLOYMENT. This graph shows how prisoner admissions to the federal prison system rise and fall according to how the national unemployment rate rises and falls. The *broken line* shows the unemployment rate, while the *solid line* shows admissions to federal prisons.

Source: NEPA News, February 1976, p. 16.

Even these figures underestimate the extent of the problem. They systematically exclude the people in the surplus population who have given up looking for jobs. Unemployment figures likewise do not count people who are employed part-time but seek full-time jobs. They also exclude the many people who are "subemployed," those who are not employed in jobs for which they are qualified. All these situations provide an employment/unemployment picture quite different from that portrayed by the government.

A way of controlling this unemployed surplus population is simply and directly by confinement in prisons. The rhetoric of criminal justice—and that of conventional criminology—is that prisons are for incarcerating criminals. In spite of this mystification, the fact is that prisons are used to control that part of the surplus population that is subject to the discretion of criminal law and the criminal justice system. What is not usually presented are the figures and the conclusion that prisons are differentially utilized according to the extent of economic crisis. The finding is clear: the prison population increases as the rate of unemployment increases. As shown in figure 3, using admissions to federal prisons, the number of prison admissions varies directly with the rate of unemployment. Unemployment simultaneously makes actions of survival and frustration necessary on the part of the unemployed surplus population and makes some form of controlling that population necessary by the state. Containment of the unemployed in prison is a certain way of controlling a threatening surplus population. Until other solutions of control are found, the capitalist state will need the certainty of the prison for controlling portions of the surplus population.

From arrest to imprisonment, then, the criminal justice system exists to control the surplus population. During

1975 the police made approximately 9.3 million arrests. This is a rate of 45 arrests for each 1,000 persons in the population. As the FBI notes in its report, "arrests are primarily a measure of police activity." [34] An attempt is being made by the police, in other words, to control the population, primarily the surplus population. While the arrest figures "provide a useful index to indicate involvement in criminal acts," they are first a measure of police activity in controlling the population. That the number of arrests has climbed, with the arrests for the major crimes increasing by over 40 percent between 1969 and the mid-1970s, is also an indication of the increasing need to control. As the economic crisis of capitalism grows, the actions generated by this crisis increase. The actions of the surplus population and the actions of the criminal justice agencies are produced by the capitalist system and are increased by the crisis in the system.

Moreover, a large portion of the population is imprisoned, and thereby controlled, at any one time.[35] The total number of prisoners in custody at the end of 1973 was 204,349 held in state and federal prisons, rising to 249,716 as of January 1, 1976. In addition to these figures there are over 45,000 juveniles held in juvenile and correctional institutions. Also there are people confined to local jails, more than half of whom have not been convicted of a

34. Federal Bureau of Investigation, *Uniform Crime Reports, 1975,* p. 37.
35. National Criminal Justice Information and Statistics Service, "Prisoners in State and Federal Institutions on December 31, 1971, 1972, and 1973," *National Prisoner Statistics Bulletin* (Washington, D.C.: U.S. Government Printing Office, 1975), p. 12; National Criminal Justice Information and Statistics Service, *Children in Custody* (Washington, D.C.: U.S. Government Printing Office, 1975), p. 8; National Criminal Justice Information and Statistics Service, *The Nation's Jails* (Washington, D.C.: U.S. Government Printing Office, 1975), p. 1.

crime. In other words, considering only the adult population, about 1 out of every 370 adults is confined at any given time to a penal institution in the United States.

Prisons in this country are used mainly for those who commit a select group of crimes, primarily burglary, robbery, larceny, and assault. Excluded are the criminals of the capitalist class, who cause more of an economic and social loss to the country and the society but who are not often given prison sentences. This means that prisons are institutions of control for the working class, especially the surplus population of the working class.

Another consequence of this use of custody and punishment is that a very large number of prisoners are black. It is estimated that 1 out of every 20 black men between the ages of 25 and 34 is either in jail or prison on any given day, compared to 1 out of every 163 white men in the same age group.[36] About one out of every four black men in their early twenties spends some time in prison, jail, or on probation. Control by the criminal justice system is indeed a reality for a good share of the American people.

The criminal justice system is nevertheless caught in the larger contradiction: late capitalism is producing a rising crime rate and the social expense of criminal justice is more than the state and the capitalist class can afford. Prisons are already dangerously overcrowded, increasing the number of "trouble-makers" within the prison and strengthening the prisoners' movement. From the standpoint of the criminal justice system, either new prisons have to be built to contain the growing number of people controlled by the system, or something has to be done to re-

36. Erik Ohlin Wright, *The Politics of Punishment: A Critical Analysis of Prisons in America* (New York: Harper & Row, 1973), pp. 31–34.

duce the size of the prison population at any single time.[37] One direction calls for the construction of roughly 1,000 new prisons, at an estimated cost of $20 billion. The other direction that the capitalist state can move is in the reduction of the prison population by means of sentencing reform.

Sentencing reforms consist mainly of mandatory, fixed, and reduced sentencing schemes. These schemes, of course, apply only to crimes committed by the working class, never the crimes of the government and the corporations. Furthermore, by reducing the length of the prison sentence, and by assuring that a prison sentence will be administered, more people can be imprisoned with certainty. This means that about 50 percent more people could be sent to prison for short terms than can now be sent for long terms.

> Viewed this way, sentencing reform is a way for the criminal justice system to have its cake and eat it too. Mandatory or fixed sentences can be introduced, sending larger numbers of people to prison while at the same time the cost of building new prisons can be avoided. Prison officials and legislators can also pose as "good guys" when shortening sentences, while also posing as "tough on crime" because more offenders will be sentenced.[38]

Prison reform actually means that control of the surplus population can be increased, for the time being at least, within the social expense limits of the criminal justice system. Future changes in control likewise will be tied to the political economy of criminal justice. Control of the surplus population is a social expense that late capitalism must

37. See the analysis in "Overcrowding and Sentence Reform," *NEPA News,* February 1976, p. 3.
38. Ibid., p. 7.

somehow meet. Built into this, of course, is a dialectic in which control is weakened in the course of class struggle and the economic crisis of the capitalist state. Criminal justice and its transformation are central to socialist revolution.

THE FUTURE OF CRIMINAL JUSTICE

The criminal justice system continues to be developed by the state and the capitalist class as a means of controlling problems (particularly the surplus population) that cannot be solved within the framework of advanced capitalism. The innovations and reforms in criminal justice are a mixture of the traditional conservative and liberal approaches to social problems, combining finally into an overall system of criminal justice. Whether the specific programs, strategies, and techniques of criminal justice are explicitly repressive and coercive, or whether they are more subtle and seemingly more humanistic, the agreed-upon purpose is a system of control for preserving late capitalism.

The direction that criminal justice is taking is indicated in the revision of the criminal code of the federal government. The proposed revision is the result of a criminal code written by the National Commission on Reform of Federal Criminal Laws and modified by subsequent amendments. In practice the new crime bill, known as S-1, provides the legal basis for further repression by the capitalist state. Included are numerous provisions, some of which are being modified in response to organized opposition:

Death Penalty: S-1 nullifies the 1972 Supreme Court decision (*Furman* v. *Georgia*) which held the death penalty unconstitutional as a form of cruel and unusual punishment.

Smith Act: S-1 revives the McCarthy-era witchhunt law that the Supreme Court, in effect, ruled unconstitutional in 1957. The bill provides 15 years' imprisonment and a $100,000 fine for mere advocacy of, or membership in, an organization that allegedly advocates revolutionary change "as speedily as circumstances permit . . . at some future time."

Rioting: S-1 redrafts the Anti-Riot Act of 1968. It calls for three years' imprisonment and a $100,000 fine for the "movement of a person across a state" line, or for the use of the mail or a telephone, "in the course of the planning or promotion" of a "riot." A "riot" is defined as "an assemblage of five" which "creates a grave danger" to "property."

Wiretapping: S-1 reaffirms the Wire-Interception Act of 1968, which permits the President to wiretap domestic activities that he thinks are a danger to the "structure" of the government.

Secrecy: S-1 provides three years in jail and a fine of $100,000 for a federal employee who "communicates . . . classified information" to an unauthorized recipient, even if the data was "not lawfully subject to classification at the time. . . ."

Sabotage: S-1 imposes penalties ranging from death to life imprisonment and 20 years in jail for activity that "damages or tampers with" almost any property, facility, or service that is or might be used in the national defense, with the intent to "interfere with or obstruct the ability of the U.S. or an associate nation (e.g., South Vietnam) to prepare for or engage in war or defense activities." In effect, the bill would subject every public demonstration, no matter how peaceful, to potential criminal sanctions.

Contempt: S-1 increases the penalty for refusal to cooperate with congressional committees to three years' imprisonment and a fine of $100,000.

Entrapment: S-1 places the burden of proof on the criminal defendant to show that he was "unlawfully entrapped," even though federal undercover agents may have provided a "facility or opportunity" and "active inducement" for the commission of the crime.[39]

Not only is state control broadened in these and other proposals, with political expression by citizens further restricted, but the state is permitted to perform criminal acts in the course of protecting the capitalist order. Even when the crimes of government agencies are exposed, as in the recent disclosures of illegal surveillance, political assassination, covert operations, and the like by the CIA and the FBI, the government response is not to prevent these criminal acts but to strengthen the agencies and the security of their secrets.[40] In fact, some current proposals, some of which can be instituted merely by executive order, give law-enforcement agencies a legal basis for domestic activities that, when conducted in the past, have been done either illegally or with questionable authority. Hence, that which the capitalist state regards as a threat to its interests and its survival is subject to control through the state's

39. Adapted from Frank Wilkinson, "The Era of Libertarian Repression—1948 to 1973: From Congressman to President, with Substantial Support from the Liberal Establishment," *University of Akron Law Review* 7 (Winter 1974): 280–309.
40. See Robert L. Borosage, "The Tyranny of 'Intelligence,'" *Nation* 222 (13 March 1976): 296–99.

own criminal (but legalized) methods. This is the nature of criminal justice under advanced capitalism.

The most ominous consequence of the revised federal code is the expansion of the jurisdiction of the federal government over crime and criminal justice. Crime control and the criminal justice system are being developed, coordinated, and increasingly administered by the federal government. As the highest level of the capitalist state, the federal government becomes the ultimate political authority in the late stages of capitalist development.

Yet, even these measures of criminal justice cannot provide an enduring solution to the problem of crime. Strengthening the criminal justice system only strengthens the larger system that generates crime in the first place. To deal with crime within the capitalist framework, by furthering legal repression, is to accept the inevitability of crime and to submit to the system that produces crime. The only real solution to crime is to be found in the class struggle. It is a political struggle against capitalism.

> We believe that real solutions to the problem of crime must begin by challenging that system itself; by moving toward programs that take power away from that system and its rulers, and transfer it to the people it now oppresses. Alternative approaches to crime must be of a kind that increase the consciousness of oppressed people and extend their ability to control their own lives. They must be linked to the broader movement to totally transform the economic and political institutions of U.S. society–the movement to build socialism in this country. In this way, the fight against crime and for a safer and more decent life can be joined with the larger struggle against the real crimes of racism, sexism, and exploitation at home and abroad.[41]

41. *The Iron Fist and the Velvet Glove*, p. 11.

The problem for us, then, is a socialist practice and a social theory that transforms criminal justice in the course of socialist revolution. As we understand the nature of criminal justice under capitalism, and as we engage in socialist struggle, we build a society that ceases to generate the crime found in capitalist society. Criminal justice ceases to be the solution to crime. Socialist solutions are to be found in the nature of the society itself—a society that neither supports nor depends on a political economy of criminal justice.

5 BEYOND CRIMINAL JUSTICE

Criminal justice—in theory and practice—is the characteristic form of control in advanced capitalist society. As the crisis in capitalism grows, however, as capitalist development reaches its final stages, even criminal justice fails to control the population. The crisis in capitalism produces at the same time a crisis in criminal justice. That new techniques of criminal justice (within the general framework of control and punishment) are constantly proposed and implemented is an indication of the increasing failure of criminal justice.

To move beyond criminal justice is to move beyond capitalism. The final development of capitalism is also the initial development of socialism. Thus, as criminal justice falters with the development of capitalism, new socialist forms of justice emerge. Rather than a justice based on the needs of the capitalist class, to the oppression of everyone else, a justice develops under socialism that satisfies the needs of the entire working class.

What is emerging as capitalist development moves to socialist development is a transformation in social, political, and economic life. We are now beginning to create the social theory and practice appropriate to socialist development. Our theory and practice necessarily go beyond that of criminal justice.

TOWARD A SOCIALIST THEORY

The notions we hold about justice (and criminal justice in particular) are themselves products of the existing mode of production. That is, under capitalism the social theory that informs our understanding of the social world is basically at the service of capital. Our knowledge and our judgments spring from the material necessities of capitalist production. As capitalism has developed, so has a theory and practice that supports capitalist development. Theory and practice today are thus shaped by an infrastructure that has as its purpose the perpetuation of capitalism. The point has been reached where science is not only a product of capitalism but itself has become a productive force. Social science, especially, is pressed into the service of capital. It has become an integral part of the accumulation process, becoming a commodity in the capitalist system.

What is needed in the transition to socialism is a social theory that supports socialist development rather than capitalist development. This is a *socialist theory* that provides the knowledge and the politics for the working class, including the surplus population, rather than knowledge for the survival of the capitalist class. In other words, the social theory appropriate for capitalism is quite different from social theory needed for socialism. Moreover, as socialism continues to develop, social theory will be modified from that necessary for the transition to socialism to that necessary for the further development of socialist society. For the moment, however, we need a social theory that allows us to move from late capitalism to the first stages of socialism.

Any science is tied to the underlying mode of production. Since the social science that we know in the capitalist world has developed within class-divided capitalist societies, our social science is predominantly a capitalist social science. And among the social sciences, as J. D. Bernal has pointed out, sociology is the science most closely tied to capitalism: "Its function has been to analyse social, political, and industrial situations in order to secure the easier running of the system. It has also had the task of explaining the system in a way that will justify and even do it credit." [1] What is needed, in contrast, is a sociology that relates to the socialist mode of production.

In the United States, where sociology has flourished since the latter part of the nineteenth century, sociology has provided the social theory required for the advancement of a social order based on an economy of industrial and monopoly capitalism. In particular, "the main current of American sociology found its ideological expression in the technocratic social reform movement and its practical expression in the production and reproduction of a social knowledge indispensable for a corporate economy's ability to contain a rebellious labor force within the capitalist mode of production and to simultaneously manage this labor force under conditions of intensive exploitation and

1. J. D. Bernal, *Science in History*, vol. 4, *The Social Sciences: Conclusion* (Cambridge, Mass.: MIT Press, 1971), p. 1209.

rapid industrial advance." [2] Rather than exploring alternatives to a capitalist social order, and providing a critique of the existing order, sociologists have tended to furnish ideas that would support the capitalist system. Even the more recent versions of sociology tend to support existing conditions instead of examining and critiquing capitalist society.[3] In being ideologically conservative, ahistorical, and situational, these sociologies fail to provide the ideas necessary for the transition to socialism.

In sharp contrast to bourgeois sociology is Marxism. Marking a divergent path, being intrinsically incompatible with bourgeois sociology, Marxism has been a force in the world for the last hundred years. Increasingly social scientists are recognizing that Marxism is the one tradition that takes as its focus the conditions of capitalist society. It is the one form of analysis that is historically specific and locates the problems of the age in the material conditions of our time. Marxism provides, moreover, a form of thought that allows us to change the world as well as understand it. The most dynamic and significant movement in the social sciences today is the development of a Marxist (or "neo-Marxist") social science. As this takes place we are creating the theory and the practice for the transition to socialism. In the process we are going beyond the capitalist notion of criminal justice.

2. Al Gedicks, "American Social Scientists and the Emerging Corporate Economy: 1885–1915," *Insurgent Sociologist* 5 (Summer 1975): 43. For a full account of the subject, see Herman Schwendinger and Julia R. Schwendinger, *The Sociologists of the Chair: A Radical Analysis of the Formative Years of North American Sociology, 1883–1922* (New York: Basic Books, 1974).
3. See Scott G. McNall and James C. M. Johnson, "The New Conservatives: Ethnomethologists, Phenomenologists, and Symbolic Interactionists," *Insurgent Sociologist* 5 (Summer 1975): 49–65.

The social science that will be a force in the movement to a socialist society and a socialist justice is one that engages all people who are struggling for a new society. Rather than being a science that justifies and assists the capitalist order, a socialist science is an integral part of the struggle for a socialist society. Already, as Bernal notes, "wherever people are coming together to criticize and oppose the oppression of class societies or colonial oppression, new kinds of social science have been growing up."[4] Moreover, socialist sciences are formed through practice:

> These begin at the other end; they are practical social sciences in which the people themselves are *changing* their social relations together with their material environment, and are discovering the principles and mode of operation of society at the same time. This is the first full social *science,* because, as in the case of the other sciences, here also it is only out of practice and through practice that a secure foundation for human knowledge can be laid.[5]

The social theory that will inform our lives will be open to all working people, instead of being the sole province of the class-derived elite who have monopolized science and social theory since the beginning of capitalist society. Academic sociology may well vanish. As in the recent Chinese experience, sociology becomes a part of the everyday culture.[6] Sociological ideas are shared by the masses of working people, produced and consumed by the people at the same time. Nevertheless: "Unlike common-sense knowledge about social life, the mass sociology is formed through scientific inquiry rather than intuition and specu-

4. Bernal, *Science in History,* p. 1026.
5. Ibid.
6. L. C. Young, "Mass Sociology: The Chinese Style," *American Sociologist* 9 (August 1974): 117–25.

lation. And needless to say, this kind of scientific knowledge is absolutely practical and well integrated with social and political practice." [7] True social theory, and a socialist sense of justice, is drawn from practical experience and verified in the everyday reality of class struggle. This takes us well beyond the capitalist theory and practice of criminal justice.

THE TRANSITION TO SOCIALISM

It is out of the final development of capitalism that socialist forms emerge. Capitalism is transformed into socialism when capitalism is no longer able to reconcile the conflicts between the existing mode of production and the relations of production, when the contradictions of capitalism reach a point where capitalism can no longer solve its own inherent problems. Ultimately capitalist relations become an obstacle to the further development of capitalism. New forms of production and social relations develop. The capitalist system finally fails to control the population; criminal justice ceases to be effective; and a new social life emerges. In other words, as another form becomes evident, socialism begins to develop. As Marx wrote:

> No social order is ever destroyed before all the productive forces for which it is sufficient have been developed, and new superior relations of production never replace older ones before the material conditions for their existence have matured within the framework of the old society. Mankind thus inevitably sets itself only such tasks as it is able to solve, since closer examination will always show that the problem itself

7. Ibid., p. 124.

> arises only when the material conditions for its solution are already present or at least in the course of formation.[8]

The material forces within capitalist society, combined with the socialist alternative, create the conditions for moving beyond the contradictions of capitalism. Thus begins the transition to socialism.

The transition to socialism is the ultimate trend of history operating within capitalist society. The transformation of capitalism to socialism thus depends on the prior development of capitalism. Socialism is nothing less than the dialectical abolition of capitalism. The development of socialism is, as Shlomo Avineri writes, "the realization of those hidden potentialities which could not have been historically realized under the limiting conditions of capitalism." [9] Capitalism creates conditions and expectations that it cannot satisfy, thus digging its own grave. At the root of the transition from capitalism to socialism is the fact that "socialism is in practice nothing but what capitalism is potentially." [10] However, since the potential cannot be satisfied under capitalism, socialism becomes necessary.

The transition to socialism does not automatically or completely dispense with the contradictions of capitalism. Some bourgeois characteristics, such as market relationships, "are inevitable under socialism for a long time, but they constitute a standing danger to the system and unless strictly hedged in and controlled will lead to degeneration and retrogression." [11] There is always the danger in transi-

8. Karl Marx, *A Contribution to the Critique of Political Economy* (New York: International Publishers, 1970), p. 21.
9. Shlomo Avineri, *The Social and Political Thought of Karl Marx* (London: Cambridge University Press, 1969), p. 150.
10. Ibid., p. 181.
11. Paul M. Sweezy and Charles Bettelheim, *On the Transition to Socialism* (New York: Monthly Review Press, 1971), p. 27.

tional societies that there will be retrogressions to former capitalist relations. For example, the problem may arise in socialist state planning:

> Without revolutionary enthusiasm and mass participation, centralized planning becomes increasingly authoritarian and rigid with resulting multiplication of economic difficulties and failures. In an attempt to solve these increasingly serious problems the rulers turn to capitalist techniques, vesting increasing power within the economic enterprises in managements and relying for their guidance and control less and less on centralized planning and more and more on the impersonal pressures of the market. Under these circumstances the juridical form of state property becomes increasingly empty and real power over the means of production, which is the essence of the ownership concept, gravitates into the hands of the managerial elite. It is this group "owning" the means of production which tends to develop into a new type of bourgeoisie, which naturally favors the further and faster extension of market relations.[12]

Within socialist society, as within capitalist society, contradictions develop that require new adaptations. The class struggle continues in the transition to socialism, and beyond to the beginning of communism.

Each transition is a unique historical process that must be understood as such. Nevertheless, all history is a continuous transformation. Even with the overthrow of class domination, with the eventual transition to communism, the transformation of human nature and social order never ceases. The disappearance of classes, the withering away of the state, the elimination of the crippling forms of the division of labor, the abolition of the distinctions between city and country and between manual and mental labor,

12. Ibid., p. 29.

even with all these, we are moved to a higher plane where other transformations become possible. As one level of human and social development is reached, another becomes evident. Out of the seeds of the past and present, our future takes shape. We move from one historical epoch to another.

An underlying force in the transition to socialism is the historical dialectic of production and labor. Late capitalism has generated new forms of labor in response to the changing requirements of capital accumulation. In order to assure continuing accumulation under advanced capitalism, the capitalist state has expanded, employing new forms of labor to carry out the work of the state apparatus. A large portion of the labor force is now involved in the dual functions of servicing (and controlling) the population and maintaining the legitimacy of the capitalist system. Work under late capitalism is both productive and unproductive in the Marxist sense. That is, while profit still continues to be appropriated through the surplus value of labor, much work is unproductive–or better, *indirectly* productive–in that the capitalist mode of production is being supported and enforced by other necessary forms of labor.

This has led some neo-Marxists to turn from a strict labor theory of value, suggesting that in the present context such activities as science and technology are the leading productive forces.[13] It is true that late capitalist development has transformed liberal capitalism into a system of welfare capitalism. The construction and implementation of a wide range of social policies is a vital feature of late capitalism. The economic and social order are sta-

13. See James Farganis, "A Preface to Critical Theory," *Theory and Society* 2 (Winter 1975): 483–508; and Peter Laska, "A Note on Habermas and the Labor Theory of Value," *New German Critique* 1 (Fall 1974): 154–62.

bilized by the capitalist state and its pervasive intervention into the economy and the population. Nevertheless, while legitimation and stabilization are secured by a large "unproductive" labor force, including (and in particular) criminal justice workers, appropriation of surplus value from the traditional productive labor force continues. The condition in late capitalism is that all labor is *production* in either the direct, surplus value sense or in the indirect, unproductive sense. The present system needs both kinds of labor in order to operate.

According to this perspective, the transition to socialism involves a dialectic between the kinds of labor needed in late capitalism. And this dialectic of labor is at the same time needed for the early development of socialism. The dialectical character of labor in production, as James O'Connor has recently argued, "is essential to a scientific understanding of the decline of capitalism and the rise of socialism." [14] The forms of labor required in the last stages of capitalist development are also part of the dialectic that moves the society to socialism. A theory of the late development of capitalism is simultaneously a theory of the transition to socialism. As O'Connor notes:

> Whatever the particular balance between productive and unproductive labor, a central problem for the analysis of capitalist economy is the determination of the conditions which create and are created by the antagonism between these two activities, an antagonism which is simply a form of the contradiction between production relations and productive forces and which historically does not come to the fore until capitalist production relations in general weaken and decay.[15]

14. James O'Connor, "Productive and Unproductive Labor," *Politics and Society* 5, no. 3 (1975): 297.
15. Ibid., pp. 318–19.

The contraction of the means of production (the means of appropriating surplus value) and the decline of the capitalist relations of production are the historical processes of capitalist decay. Late capitalism demands an ever increasing "unproductive" labor force to maintain the overall capitalist system. As this indirectly productive labor force increases, the appropriation of surplus value (necessary for capitalist accumulation) decreases. Surplus value as the source of capital accumulation declines at the expense of maintaining the capitalist system. This is the grave, and fatal, contradiction of late capitalism.

The new forms of unproductive labor under late capitalism are simultaneously the source of presocialist or early socialist labor. A noncapitalist mode of production is being generated by late capitalism. Unproductive labor heightens the contradiction of capitalist development. Moreover, the increasing contradiction provides a source for the development of an awareness among workers of the true nature of capitalist labor. Eventually, out of the recognition of the alienation and exploitation of capitalist labor, and given the appropriate historical conditions, there is the development of *socialist* productive forces. Thus, O'Connor writes, "socialist labor seeks to use the means and objects of production to produce use values directly for need, not exchange values, i.e., socialist labor seeks to control, mold, and shape things, not people." [16] Socialist labor requires consciousness, a critique of capitalist labor, and a knowledge of the productive forces of socialism.

> If we define the productive forces as the worker's knowledge of production and distribution and energy and imagination (as well as the means and objects of production), then we can say that socialist labor is the abolition of the capitalist

16. Ibid., p. 332.

> production relations by the productive forces. It is the transformation by the producing class itself of itself from historical object to subject. In this general light, the difference between productive labor and socialist labor is the difference between a working class which (necessarily) permits itself to be used like a machine and a class which is able to take its destiny into its own hands.[17]

In the historical movement from capitalism to socialism, workers are engaged in the struggle for the liberation of the working class.

Accompanying the change in historical conditions, therefore, is the development of working-class consciousness. While working-class consciousness does not automatically follow changes in the objective conditions, class consciousness is necessary if the socialist transition is to be fully realized. Needed are working-class institutions that are part of the struggle to produce socialist relations.[18] Rather than the reproduction of a capitalist ideology that merely supports capitalist decay, the development of a socialist consciousness that directs the development of socialism is necessary. Whether as a party, a workplace council, or a grass-roots movement, a working-class consciousness appropriate for the transition to socialism is formed in the class struggle that occurs in the historical and concrete period of late capitalism.

It is not only the capitalist economy that is to be surmounted in the transition to socialism but the capitalist state as well. The state under advanced capitalism plays the crucial role of political coordination for the society as a whole. The capitalist state maintains a symbiotic–but increasingly tenuous–relationship with the political econ-

17. Ibid., p. 335.
18. See Richard Lichtman, "Marx's Theory of Ideology," *Socialist Revolution* 5 (April 1975): 45–76.

omy of late capitalism. Today the capitalist state has attained a semiautonomous position. Under late capitalism the economy is as much dependent on the capitalist state as the state is dependent on the economy.

In the final stage of capitalist development the state and the economy may well become antagonistic. Already, for example, monopoly capital is forming into multinational corporations in order to bypass intervention by the national state. The point may be reached (or is already being reached) where advanced capitalism poses a threat to the continued existence of the state. A real tension is developing between the economy of late capitalism and the interests of the modern state. The antagonism opens the way for socialist struggle. A socialist economy as well as a socialist state is in the making.

That a socialist state will be necessary in the first stages of socialism follows from socialist theory. Socialist society will require direction and planning, since socialism implies the subjection of human creative powers to conscious direction.[19] Yet, as Marx argues, while the state represents the attempt to realize human ideals politically, solutions must be found beyond the state. Eventually the dichotomy between state and civil society will disappear. In concrete terms of historical reality, the dialectic between the state and civil society will be worked out in various ways, differing from one society to another and from one stage of socialism to another. Avineri thus makes the following Marxian observation:

> Since the future is not as yet an existing reality, any discussion of it reverts to philosophical idealism in discussing objects which exist only in the consciousness of the thinking subject. Marx's discussions of future society are therefore

19. Avineri, *The Social and Political Thought of Karl Marx*, pp. 202–7.

> more austere and restrained. He never tried to rival those socialists whom he called utopian by construing detailed blue-prints for a communist society, since for him communist society will be determined by the specific conditions under which it is established and these conditions cannot be predicted in advance. One can only attempt to delineate some of the dominant features of future society, and even this is very cautiously and tentatively done.[20]

In general, however, in the first stage of socialism private property will be abolished by turning it into universal property, the property of all.[21] Workers will be in control of production as well as owning the means of production. Decisions about collective endeavors will be made democratically, as true democracy can exist only under socialism. With subsequent developments there will be an end to domination by the objective forces of our existence. This can occur only after the birth pangs of the creation of the new society. We are then free to transcend our objective conditions, no longer limited by the alienation and restrictions of a former age. "Under such a system man's relation to nature ceases to be determined by objective necessity: man, now conscious of his mastery over nature, creates it." [22] Such is possible with the proper organization of our creative powers. Human conditions of life can now be controlled by human consciousness instead of consciousness being determined by the objective forces of circumstance.

This takes us far beyond criminal justice. To transcend the capitalist economy and the capitalist state is also to transcend criminal justice. In the transition to socialism there is a dialectic between criminal justice and a popular

20. Ibid., p. 221.
21. Ibid., pp. 223–29.
22. Ibid., p. 227.

justice movement beyond the control of the state. Developing consciousness among the working class involves a consciousness about social control. Working-class institutions will create forms of dealing with the problems that accompany class struggle, including protection from the repression of the capitalist state. These forms will be in the hands of the working class, not in the jurisdiction of the state. The forms of control and human transformation will become apparent only in the movement toward socialism and in the movement from one stage of socialism to another. The only thing we can be certain of now is that the forms of "justice"—or whatever the conceptualization that will be created—will be appropriate to the emerging society. The movement is clearly beyond criminal justice.

THEORY AND PRACTICE

People make their own history, Marx noted, "but they do not make it just as they please; they do not make it under circumstances chosen by themselves, but under circumstances directly encountered, given and transmitted from the past." [23] The desire alone for change is not a sufficient condition for socialist revolution. Rather, the objective, material conditions of the time provide the setting for the possibilities of change. Furthermore, only with the actions of real, living human beings struggling against the oppressive conditions of capitalism can there be a socialist revolution. With class consciousness, in concrete historical circumstances, people act politically to bring about a new society.

23. Karl Marx, *The Eighteenth Brumaire of Louis Bonaparte* (New York: International Publishers, 1963), p. 15.

The problem of correct political action for socialist revolution involves a unity of theory and practice. Theory without practice not only makes bad theory but also shuts off the possibility of actual political struggle. On the other hand, practice without theory leads to incorrect action for socialist revolution. The only way to solve the problem is to combine social theory and social practice. The process is a never-ending one, being subject to reformulations of both theory and practice in the transformation. In his elaborate analysis of the subject, Mao Tse-tung describes the process as follows:

> The discovery of truths through practice, and their verification and development through practice; the active development of perceptual knowledge into rational knowledge, and, by means of rational knowledge, the active direction of revolutionary practice and the reconstruction of the subjective and the external world; practice, knowledge, more practice, more knowledge, and the repetition *ad infinitum* of this cyclic pattern, and with each cycle the elevation of the content of practice and knowledge to a higher level–such is the whole epistemology of dialectical materialism, such is its theory of the unity of knowledge and action.[24]

The problem of combining theory and practice is especially acute in those areas of knowledge that explicitly claim to provide theory for action–namely, the social sciences. As the social sciences developed within the capitalist hegemony, the theory of social science furnished a practice that supported the state and political economy of capitalism. A new social theory, however, one that develops outside capitalist interests, provides a knowledge and a politics that moves us toward a socialist society. A socialist social theory

24. Mao Tse-tung, *On Practice* (New York: International Publishers, n.d.), pp. 15–16.

necessarily emerges out of the practice of socialist revolution.

The socialist idea of the unity of *theory* and *practice* obviously differs from the current, positivist (and capitalist) notion of social science and social policy. The "policy sciences," as they are sometimes called, provide a social engineering model of change.[25] Courses of action are suggested by the policy scientist in terms of available technical information and according to the needs of the existing arrangements of the society. In other words, policy science rationalizes capitalist society. The practice that is offered, by and for the professional and political elite, is that of technical control.

A critical social theory, in contrast, is grounded in the social life of those who are oppressed by existing conditions. The purpose of critical social theory is not to manipulate people, but rather "to enlighten the social actors so that, coming to see themselves and their social situation in a new way, they themselves can decide to alter the conditions which they find repressive." [26] In other words, social theory is for the development of consciousness through self-reflection and an understanding of the objective conditions. This leads the way to collective actions that will change the existing social order. "According to the critical model of social science," Brian Fay writes, "a social theory does not simply offer a picture of the way that a social order works; instead, a social theory is itself a catalytic agent of change within the complex of social life which it analyses." [27]

A theory and practice by and for the working class is

25. Brian Fay, *Social Theory and Political Practice* (London: George Allen & Unwin, 1975), pp. 18–69.
26. Ibid., p. 103.
27. Ibid., p. 110.

aimed at liberation and emancipation rather than at the domination of nature and other human beings. Bourgeois social science–with the possession of technical capabilities –attempts to dominate and control other people, mainly those who labor. Logically and historically, the domination of nature and humanity is linked to capitalist society.[28] The bourgeois social science of capitalist society is at the service of the capitalist class. Socialist social theory, in contrast, being created by the working class in struggle, seeks to remove class oppression and place the determination of life in the hands of those who actually produce.

Thus bourgeois social science aids in the control of the population, especially under the guise of criminal justice. Criminology, in particular, has long been an ancillary agent of capitalist order. The theory and research of bourgeois criminology, or in the new field of "criminal justice," assists in the manipulation and control of the working class. A Marxist criminology, in contrast, is attempting to go beyond the criminal justice emphasis of bourgeois criminology. It is allied to the popular struggles against capitalist oppression and for the creation of a socialist society.

Replacing the bourgeois notion of criminal justice is the idea of *popular justice*.[29] In the late stage of capitalist development this means that people are attempting to resolve conflicts between themselves in their own communities and workplaces. Outside the legal institutions of the capitalist

28. William Leiss, *The Domination of Nature* (Boston: Beacon Press, 1974), pp. 101–23.
29. Popular justice in the United States and in socialist countries is being investigated and documented by the Popular Justice Research Group, of the Boston Union of Radical Criminologists. The group consists of, in addition to myself, John Baumann, James Brady, Alexander Liazos, and Richard Speiglman. I would like to acknowledge my indebtedness to this group of friends, and to thank them for their assistance and support.

state, people are trying to deal with their own problems collectively, according to their own terms. Popular justice is an alternative to the criminal justice of the capitalist state. It is also being used as a tool in the class struggle. Working-class people are being educated as to the class nature of contemporary society.

With the transition to socialism, popular justice may become institutionalized into the society and the state. Already in such socialist countries as China and Cuba, popular justice institutions have been created and supported by the state. These institutions protect and solidify the working class against internal and external class enemies, as well as against elitist bureaucratic tendencies in the state apparatus. The long-term use and fate of popular justice, as we progress to communism, are far from certain. The experiences will differ from one society to another. Only in the struggle and the transformation will future forms become evident.

A critical understanding of criminal justice as practiced in capitalist society is a necessary condition for moving beyond the theory and practice of criminal justice, indeed, for the movement to a socialist society. A theoretical analysis of the structure of criminal justice in relation to the structure of capitalist economy is in itself a revolutionary praxis. The role of theory in practical action will not vanish under socialism. On the contrary, social theory will be even more important than under capitalism, in that social theory will become a part of the everyday life for the masses of people. If a social science remains, it will be one that belongs to the working class rather than a social science practiced by the capitalist class against the workers.

The purpose of social theory–including a critical understanding of criminal justice–in the transition to socialism is to subvert the capitalist hegemony that maintains its hold over the working class. Socialist social theory provides people with an understanding of their alienation and oppressed condition, and provides a means of expression that is the beginning of socialist revolution.[30] To engage in social theory under these conditions is to engage in ideological, educational, and practical work. Social theory assists in the development of class consciousness. As Theotonio Dos Santos observes: "The intellectual, considered not as an individual isolated in an ivory tower but as a militant intellectual of a class, is thus a key factor in working out and developing class consciousness." [31] A conscious working-class culture of emancipation is created.

For those who engage in this work, bourgeois ways of social science must necessarily be transcended. Social theorists, whose work has the character of critical inquiry, must be "capable of moving across the boundaries of normal science with its normal division of labor." [32] In rejecting the boundaries of normal scholarship and bourgeois paradigms, the existing order is critically examined and the socialist alternative proposed. Embodied within critique and proposal is a politics of working-class struggle and socialist revolution.

Social theory, then, is to serve the working class in the struggle for a socialist society. As bourgeois social theory serves the capitalist class under capitalism, socialist social theory serves the working class under socialism and assists in the transition to socialism. In the struggle, social theory is constantly revised and practice is altered to better achieve

30. André Gorz, *Socialism and Revolution* (New York: Doubleday, 1973), pp. 170–74.
31. Theotonio Dos Santos, "The Concept of Social Class," *Science and Society* 34 (Summer 1970): 186.
32. Alvin W. Gouldner, "Prologue to a Theory of Revolutionary Intellectuals," *Telos,* no. 26 (Winter 1975–76): 23.

the goal of a socialist society. The only purpose in knowing the world, as Mao notes, is to change it.[33]

In understanding criminal justice–its theory and practice under capitalism–we provide a theory and a practice that has as its objective changing the world. The importance of criminal justice is that it moves us dialectically to reject the capitalist order and to struggle for a new society. We are engaged in socialist revolution.

33. Mao Tse-tung, *Where Do Correct Ideas Come From?* (Peking: Foreign Languages Press, 1966), p. 3. Also, on the role of intellectual workers, see Mao Tse-tung, *Speech at the Chinese Community Party's National Conference on Propaganda Work* (Peking: Foreign Languages Press, 1968).